WILLA CATHER IN EUROPE

Other writings by Willa Cather published by the
University of Nebraska Press

Alexander's Bridge

April Twilights
Revised Edition, edited and with an introduction by Bernice Slote

The Kingdom of Art:
Willa Cather's First Principles and Critical Statements, 1893–1896
Selected and edited with two essays and a commentary by Bernice Slote

Not Under Forty

The Troll Garden
A Definitive Edition, edited by James Woodress

Uncle Valentine and Other Stories:
Willa Cather's Uncollected Short Fiction, 1915–1929
Edited and with an introduction by Bernice Slote

Willa Cather's Collected Short Fiction, 1892–1912
*Revised Edition, edited by Virginia Faulkner with an introduction by
Mildred R. Bennett*

Willa Cather in Person:
Interviews, Speeches, and Letters
Selected and edited by L. Brent Bohlke

Willa Cather on Writing
Critical Studies on Writing as an Art

The World and the Parish:
Willa Cather's Articles and Reviews
Selected and edited with a commentary by William M. Curtin

WILLA CATHER
in Europe

Her Own Story of the First Journey

With an Introduction
and Incidental Notes by
George N. Kates

University of Nebraska Press
Lincoln and London

First Bison Book printing: 1988
Most recent printing indicated by the first digit below:

1   2   3   4   5   6   7   8   9   10

Library of Congress Cataloging-in-Publication Data
Cather, Willa, 1873–1947.
    Willa Cather in Europe: her own story of the first journey / with
an introduction and incidental notes by George N. Kates.
        p.   cm.
    "First Bison book printing."
    Reprint. Originally published: New York: A.A. Knopf, 1956.
    ISBN 0-8032-6333-3 (pbk.)
    1. Cather, Willa, 1873–1947—Journeys—Europe. 2. England—
Description and travel—1901–1945. 3. France—Description and
travel—1800–1918. 4. Novelists, American—20th century—Jour-
neys—Europe. I. Kates, George N. (George Norbert), 1895–
II. Title.
PS3505.A87Z476   1988
818′.5203—dc19
[B]   CIP 88-1125

Published by arrangement with Alfred A. Knopf, Inc.

INTRODUCTION

Not often are we given an opportunity to observe a great American writer arrive for the first time in the Old World from the New, there to record first impressions spontaneously, as they came, subject to no second thoughts, no later, leveling revision. The fourteen travel articles that form the present volume, written by Willa Cather on a first journey to England and France, give us just such a record. They were made for pay, jotted down quickly, often in obvious haste, and then apparently sent back just as they were to the *Nebraska State Journal*, in Lincoln. There they were set up in print, also with no special care, to fill a weekly column or two of the local paper.

1902 was the Edwardian year when Willa Cather, with her friend Isabelle McClung, proceeded on this journey. We can follow them as they go, from Liverpool to Chester and Shrewsbury, to Ludlow and the quiet Shropshire country; onward into the dim vastness of London—which almost overwhelmed her by its contrast with anything she had met before—then further across the Channel to other skies, to Rouen, Paris, and the Midi.

In this summer Willa Cather was still only twenty-eight. Her writing career, at least in terms of books, still lay wholly ahead of her. She had been teaching English and Latin in one of the high schools of Pittsburgh, and she was to go back to her classes after this vacation. Even her first slim volume of poetry, *April Twilights*, was to appear only in the following year. As we shall see, it bears more than one mark of this journey.

The interest of the present material—in spite of all its marks of unplanned and unorganized writing—is double. We shall of course first catch impressions, fresh, as they occurred. Then, subsequently, we shall be able to trace their development through a whole career. Some seed fell on barren ground. Certain subjects here loom large; and later never appear again. Others, indistinguishable from them, perhaps, were we not in the privileged position of knowing a future still unrevealed to the author herself, are to grow from this summer of 1902 until after many years they will become the main themes of her matured and finest work.

Step by step we here can see a country-bred girl, a young schoolteacher who except for a few years in Pittsburgh had known only early childhood in rural Virginia, and then an untrammeled life growing up in the developing West, make her first experiences amid all the heaped-up riches, the accumulated treasure, of European civilization, feeling deeply its weight and glory, its past and present.

For much of what she thus was to confront, Willa Cather was by no means unprepared. She was, we know, unusually well read, in several literatures, even for a generation more serious about such matters than we are in general today. She was properly grounded, also, in her knowledge of European art. Her classical education had included both Greek and Latin; as enjoyments, moreover, rather than as disciplines. We shall find her on terms of easy familiarity with the lives of poets like de Musset and Heine. She has made a cult of Flaubert; she is an enthusiastic admirer of A. E. Housman for some time before his reputation is made. As spectators we can watch the precious moments of first revelation, the excitements, the joys, as one by one she discovers traces of their lives, here on their native soil. These were major confrontations; and they sank in for life.

The creative process is highly mysterious. As spectators, we have of course a great advantage. We are able to move up and down the time scale of her career at will, following vital processes from their first germination here in these rapidly tossed-off pages, through curious transformations, even through silent and subterranean development, into permanent form, often achieved only many years later. We can, moreover, observe this development long before she herself could have been aware of what was happening.

What later was to become, even for Europe, "the precious, the incommunicable past" is here merely the fleeting present, seen with fresh eyes, fresh energies, and fresh talents. Here speaks youth, a youth she would try hard to overlay with maturity before she felt emboldened to transform into verse or prose what she had found. Certain colors of the palette are tried here—we can trace them—never to be used again. Some scenes, the magical effect of certain places, will only grow in intensity, in depth and significance, as long as life endures. Her unexpected love for the Midi is an example. We can watch instinct at work long before it was to reveal itself. There are suggestions on every page.

The roughnesses, the occasional immaturity, are of minor importance. What matters is the inspiration, the great individuality of the impression. So much in

these sketches is young, active, vigorous, and compe-
tent. There are plenty of provincialisms, of Americanisms, even those of 1902. Much seems improvised,
even at the moment of impact in revelatory travel. Yet
the reader will also find passages that are a foretaste of
her highest style, passages of unchallengeable beauty
and power. These he may wish to select for himself;
her description of a world transformed, during the
night crossing from England to France, however, or
her contrast of unreal and unsatisfactory Monte Carlo
with nourishing Provence, are typical examples.

It is also interesting to see what was *not* used later!
Her curiosity about the arrangement of Parisian cemeteries, for example, at least as a formal setting, seems
to have been quite transitory. Liverpool, Chester, and
Ludlow, at the beginning of the journey, yielded to far
more interesting places as it progressed. All is nevertheless a prefiguration, part of a wonderful and vital
record, pregnant with creation to come.

A few words may here be in place about the text itself. It shows many marks of haste, there is often loose
grammar, obvious repetition. Indeed, there are so
many superficial imperfections that one can only de-
duce real impatience, at times, to fulfill a set task while
new life was calling, with high allurement, on every

hand. One also fancies that the uninstructed local compositor, in Nebraska—no doubt reading hastily written copy—often has only added further error.

Titles to each article have been added; although dates are as Willa Cather gave them. Spellings and occasional punctuation have been standardized; and there have also been made a few occasional small changes necessary for sense. These last, though, were decided upon merely to make casual reading easier. No crudities were erased, no repetitious language improved upon.

Here, then, without embellishment, and now with the perspective of over half a century, we can secure glimpses of Willa Cather's youth, of high aspiration, of seriousness and honor. This is a record of early enthusiasms, on a wonderful first journey to taste of the riches of the world.

What general conclusions can we draw from this miscellaneous material? First, I think, we can see Willa Cather slowly choosing—often by experiment that tells her chiefly in what directions she could *not* go—the types of people she will write about. The conventional world does not draw her; she is not at home in it, no matter where she finds it. Yet it will take her some time before she can walk confidently into those regions, here clearly foreshadowed, where her interest was held.

This is also true of her choice of subject. At the beginning she still tries traditional themes, conventional forms. In *April Twilights* we shall find verses on "Paris," the "Mills of Montmartre," or "Poppies on Ludlow Castle," modeled upon familiar styles. Yet even in this first little book they alternate with more original and more American subjects, such as "The Night Express" and "Prairie Dawn," an earnest of the larger swing necessary, in both her first stories and novels, before she could determine her range.

Finally there is the setting. This follows the same evolution: we shall progress from the conventional, the worldly, more and more to her own "native" material, toward subjects nobody had ever used for fiction before. Finally, of course, she will be able to use both at will, even juxtaposing them, with a peculiar sensitiveness wholly her own. Thus, in *Death Comes for the Archbishop* she sets Santa Fe, in its desert country, at her desired remove from Europe by beginning the action on a terrace in Rome, early in the last century. She also contrived a similar effect of counterpoint in *Shadows on the Rock*, where the story begins in grave, primitive Quebec with the arrival up the St. Lawrence of a sailing ship from the distant shores of seventeenth-century France. These are examples of her full-fledged technique, however; into the air of the Divide, again and again, she enjoys putting another temporary vibration, for fleeting contrast, often evoking it with the mere mention of a distant city, of Bergen or of Prague.

Her interest in the meaning of Europe grew steadily; the permanent values of life in the Old World became always more important. We know now that at the end of her career this American writer actually moved back, in imagination, first to a place like Aix-les-Bains, in "The Old Beauty"; and finally, in her last and uncompleted story, to medieval Avignon—this time with no return.

Now, though, we have witnessed a full curve of development, through a career that had lasted a lifetime. All the more precious, then, are these vigorous and sincere, quite unrevised impressions, of people, of incidents, and of places, at the beginning of the journey.

George N. Kates

Santa Fe
April 1956

CONTENTS

WILLA CATHER IN EUROPE

[1]

Liverpool

Willa Cather first touched the Old World, at a commercial port, in unexpected circumstances. At the end of June in 1902, as she and her friend Isabelle McClung were debarking, the whole of Britain was remaking plans, trying to digest news of the quite unexpected illness of Edward VII, on the very eve of his coronation. This had thrown into sudden confusion elaborate plans, throughout the nation, for a festival. They found the whole city still garlanded and flag-bedecked; although the great celebration had now to be postponed indefinitely. Parts of it, nevertheless, were to be carried through; and into these local proceedings the two women were promptly gathered.

Thus absorbing first uneven impressions, among the idle crowds, it is the appearance of the working people that strikes her. Their whole standard is deplorable; their clothing "frankly a shock at first." Poverty she was familiar with; but such slatternliness, and the decrepitude, are new. The carriage of the women, in particular, she finds dreadful. She strikes out in vigorous protest at their dowdy, unbecoming clothing, their unbelievable hats, their cheap jewelry. There are also puzzling contrasts. Where place amidst this, for example, the gentle English voices?

During her first afternoon she somehow attends a public feast for the aged poor, which it had been decided not to cancel. Here she finds one grim detail after another. Her fascinated observation of the dregs of the community is typical. It is also an earnest not only of the kinds of people she will notice throughout her journey, but of those she will later prefer to write about; nearly all of them marked, as she puts it, by a real "tussle with poverty."

So we find her launched in England, into quite another world than the one she may have expected. Everyone seems to have been bemused by the universal change of plans; yet it was an odd and unanticipated introduction, into a world not of beauty but of realism.

Reverting to the uncrowned new King, so much in people's thoughts during these very hours, to close this first article she essays a brief sketch, concise and well phrased, of the thankless life she divines that he has had to live—quite contrary to his common reputation in America—during the long years of his domineering mother's flinty old age. Here it is the human situation, rather than the political, that has drawn her interest.

Liverpool, July 1, 1902

ON the 26th of June Liverpool presented such an array of colour, flowers, and banners as very nearly disguised the grimness of the city itself. We arrived at about eight o'clock of the most radiant of June mornings, and our drive to the Northwestern Hotel was under canopies, arches, and flags. From pillar to pillar along the sidewalks ran chains of paper roses for miles. Everywhere hung pictures of the King and Queen. The shops were all closed, and workingmen were standing about the streets, yet there was a palpable shadow in the air that did not belong to a festival. Even had the news of the King's illness not reached us at Queenstown, we would certainly have recognized symptoms of discomfiture in the streets of Liverpool. Moreover, in hundreds of places the silk draperies which bore the inscription "God Save the King" and been torn down and others substituted with the legend "God Raise Our King."

The Northwestern Hotel, at which my friend and I stopped, is directly opposite the public square and St. George's Hall, which is by far the finest building in Liverpool. The square was a sheet of blazing sunshine that morning, and the Union Jack everywhere fluttered and tugged in the wind. A blind man with a concertina played national airs at the foot of a colossal statue of the Duke of Wellington, that stands on a column 115 feet high. The "bobbies" were lined up on the steps of St. George's Hall, and a few redcoats, with their caps perched at their favourite jaunty angle, and short canes under their arms, came and went among the groups of people who thronged the square. A group of girls with their hair hanging loose over their shoulders, and the most strident voices imaginable, sold flowers at the foot of an equestrian statue, done in bronze by Thornycroft when the Empress was a young woman.

Although the whole effect was remarkably gay, there was nothing of the smartness and neatness and trimness of an American crowd. The square as a whole presented a beautiful variation of line and colour, but the majority of the individuals who made up these dark splotches on the yellow plane were far from lovely. The dress of English women, and of English men of the working class, is frankly a shock at first, no matter how catholic one may be in such matters. I have been in England a week now, and I have not seen one English girl or woman of the middle class who is not stoop-shouldered to a painful degree, or who does not stand with her chest sunk in and the lower part of the torso thrust forward. Even in the little, little girls one sees the beginning of it—the topping of the shoulders and contraction of the chest. This unfortunate carriage is so universal that it amounts to a national disfigurement among the women. Girls with the skin of a rose, and well-featured enough, have the figures of riddled old dames. Their dress is almost as remarkable. The American idea of neatness, of being genuine as far as you go, of having little and having it good, which at home even the shop girls imbibe more or less of, prevails not at all here. The streets are always full of badly made, home-concocted silks and satins and lawns and dimities. No shirtwaist is complete without a daub of penny lace on it, no skirt is correct unless it trails in the back, is too short in front, and is a cascade of draggled ruffles and flounces. The railway trains are full of young women travelling in white muslin, white stockings, and white shoes. Their hats are something beyond belief. Hats have never at all been one of the vexing problems of my life, but, indifferent as I am, these render me speechless. I should think a well-taught and tasteful American milliner would go mad in England, and eventually hang herself with bolts of green and scarlet ribbon—the favourite colour combination in Liverpool. The flower girls have nothing in their trays half as brilliant as the blossoms on their bonnets. The English working girl, and especially the country girl, has a passion for cheap jewellery. She wears the most unblushing frauds of the sort, even to the extent of half a dozen breastpins at once. However, I am not at all sure that I would be willing to exchange the pretty voice. After hearing only English voices for a few days, the first American voice you hear in a boarding-house is very apt to suggest something of the nature of burrs or sandpaper.

On the afternoon of the 26th we went to see the poor of Liverpool fed at St. George's Hall, just across the street. The lord mayor and lord mayoress had arranged to dine all the worthy aged poor there, in honour of the new King's ascent to the throne; and in accordance to the King's wish that all the coronation festivities in which the poor were to receive gratuities should be carried out, the great dinner was given on

the day set for it. There were over five hundred guests
entertained in all, each of the guests being over sixty
years old, and some upwards of ninety. The dinner
consisted of roast beef, vegetables, plum pudding,
beer. As the guests left the hall, they were each presented with packages of tea and sugar, and the men
with plugs of tobacco. While the old folks were eating, Mr. Roberts, organist of St. Paul's, played the
coronation march written by Mackenzie for the coronation of Edward VII, and afterward "Zadock, the
Priest," one of the suite of four numbers written by
Handel for the coronation of George II and Queen
Caroline.

Constant comparisons are the stamp of the for-
eigner; one continually translates manners and customs of a new country into the terms of his own, before he can fully comprehend them. There are so
many thoroughly engaging and attractive things about
English life and people that it is not a little satisfaction to be able to say to oneself that in no American
city could be nurtured such an array of poverty and
decrepitude as filed into St. George's Hall on that holi-
day. They seemed worn to the bone, some of them,
and all of them had had a sixty years' tussle with poverty in a land where the competition is exceedingly
close. There was very little sullenness, however; they

seemed as eager and pleased as children; and as the caterer's men, all in white duck, carried huge cauldrons up the street and into the side door, the long file of poor inhaled the savoury odour from the kettles with smiling satisfaction.

Every old dame who had a red rag of a flower in her black bonnet was happy. The tickets which admitted guests to the hall had been distributed by the vestry-men and the guardians of the poor. Of course a great number of people arrived who had no tickets, hulks of drunken old sailors, whom you see everywhere in Liver-pool, poor old women, who had, every one, an excuse, but never a ticket when the cooks and the cauldrons arrived, and the odour of the food whetted their appe-tites. Some of them became quite desperate, and tried by every means to smuggle themselves into the happy ticket line, fairly clawing at the bobbies, who gently put them back. Some sat down on the steps and cried bitterly into their aprons; some railed upon the false-ness and futility of human institutions in general. When we came out from the hall half an hour later, they were still there, held by the tantalizing odour; scolding, crying, sulking, so old and tired and poor that one's heart went out to them who had not on the wedding garment. The cause of their misfortune was not apparent; perhaps they were professional beggars;

perhaps they had bad records behind them; but their age was evident enough, and their hunger, and when at last the bobbies drove them even from the steps, one could not help regretting their defeat.

The feeling of sympathy for the King seems to be a very genuine one. Most English people think he has not been altogether justly used. They believe Queen Victoria should have abdicated twenty years ago, when she retired to nurse her private sorrow. These twenty years, they say, Edward has been doing the sovereign's work, with none of the sovereign's perquisites. The evidence seems to be very much against the American notion that the King's life has been one rosy path of wine and song. A detailed account of the daily routine the King has gone through for the last twenty years rather staggers one. He embodies many of those qualities which the English people esteem most highly. He is a good sportsman, he can do a great deal of work without making any display, his personal courage is as unquestioned as his generosity. Even his extravagant taste for boxing and the turf endears him, not only to the smart world, but to the common people as well. His son, the present Prince of Wales, is the antithesis of his father, and is exceedingly unpopular. He is said to be foppish and effeminate to the last degree.

[2]

Chester and Its Cathedral

This second article, sent back to Nebraska from more rural England, shows Willa Cather still at the beginning of her European education. It bears every mark of hasty writing, perhaps even without revision before it was submitted to the local paper. It is easy to see where she has inserted a date, or culled a legend—no doubt from some convenient guidebook—simply because at the beginning she may have felt that these were expected from her. The style is at times raw, with a generous sprinkling of Americanisms, and no mastery as yet of a vocabulary necessary, for example, to describe good architecture.

The venerable age, the inevitable "quaintness" of her surroundings obviously first impress her; but even here she soon begins to discover her own material. Not for her were great houses, even that of the Duke of Westminster. To this she gives a single sentence! It is the "dwellings of the common people" that make in her mind the charm of an old town like Chester; and this she tells us promptly. She also notices every growing thing, as she was to do throughout life. A happy enumeration begins in the first paragraph of this article.

Typically also, here in Cheshire, she seems at once to have devised her own highly individual manner of sightseeing. Avid as she is for the full force of new and important impressions, she apparently never makes—nor was later to make—any attempt at completeness of coverage, at the systematic seeing of many things. On the contrary, with her friend we find her from the beginning spending her time just as she wants to, "lying a morning through at the foot of the Norman tower," for example, of the Old Castle at Hawarden. These are the precious hours of a young schoolteacher's vacation, her first in Europe; yet we find her thus passing "half of a June day in almost utter solitude," contemplating time past and gone.

It is values such as these that she has come to garner; quality—not multiplicity. Throughout this journey, we shall discover, whenever Willa Cather finds something of personal interest, she inevitably goes to it directly, intensely, in all simplicity, forgetting rather than forgoing other appeals. So even in Cheshire, she looks at the small houses with their walled gardens, which have appealed to her imagination; or she dallies long in the grass beneath an ancient tower, taking her time to plummet its meaning.

Gradually, though, the larger lines loom: this is typical of her process of assimilation. She mentions the cathedral last, not first; and even with it she will begin by considering small bits of its history, how it was planned by Saint Anselm for Hugh Lupus, or how the first Norman church on the site was arranged to house Saint Werburgh's remains, but then was "built over and under and around"—down the centuries.

In the end, though, something much larger rises before her "eyes of unfaith." She begins to apprehend the fuller meaning of the old pre-Reformation Europe, to see medieval Catholic life as a whole, in its order and its beauty. The cathedral cloister, in light and shadow, grants her this vision; and gives her the perfect place in which to dream. So we find her spending afternoons in its "utter peacefulness," gradually divining what a great and secular tradition can do to shape a culture.

This ultimate value, this outsider's warm approach

to Catholic faith, will come to full expression only more than a quarter-century later in her two novels most concerned with religion, Death Comes for the Archbishop, published in 1927, and Shadows on the Rock, of 1931; although the meditation first evoked here in an English medieval cloister will continue even to the end of her life. The development from Chester to Santa Fé and Quebec, and then on to her last, unfinished story, which she was later to set even in the Palace of the Popes in Avignon, is clear. We are present at its inception.

Chester, July 1, 1902

CHESTER, which is considered the quaintest and most picturesque of all English towns, is about fifteen miles from Liverpool on the river Dee, in the region where the sand-bars are wide and the tide treacherous, and where the fishermen still hear Mary calling her cattle home. The town is planted at the foot of the wildest of the Welsh hills, and is one of the oldest in England. In the business part of the town the streets are nearly all called "Rows"—that is, the second story of each building is built over the side walls and forms a sort of roof, being supported by heavy posts. Many of these buildings have endured from Elizabeth's time, some are even older, and when new ones are built they are put up in exactly the same manner. The dwellings are many of them very handsome, especially Eaton Hall, the summer place of the Duke of Westminster, which lies about six miles out. The chief charm of the town, however, lies in the dwellings of the common people. They are quaint red brick houses, the majority of them very old, with diamond window-panes and high-walled gardens behind. These high walls, the red brick beautifully toned and coloured by age and overgrown with ivy, tea vines, and Virginia creepers, form one of the chief beauties of these gardens. A hedge of holly or alder trees often rises even above the wall, which is seldom less than twenty-five feet high. Then there is always the matchless English green of the sod, the gravel walks, the fern bed, poppies, and pale iris growing next the wall, and the apple and pear tree, under which the family take their afternoon tea.

The walls of Chester mark the boundaries of the old city, though now they simply form an oblong in the middle of the town. The exact date of their erection is not known, but they were probably built in the reigns of Elizabeth and James, on the site of the walls of the mediæval town. They are of red sandstone and are about thirty feet high. A rail has been put along one side, and the top of the wall is now used as a promenade and forms a delightful walk from which you can look down into the walled gardens. The whole circuit of the old walls is about two miles. At the northeast corner is the Phœnix Tower, from which Charles I witnessed the defeat of his troops on Rowton Moor, just outside the town walls. Before the arrival of the King, the city, which was one of the most loyal in the west, had stood a long siege by the Parliamentarians. The citizens were reduced to eating all their cats and dogs, and every silver coin was cut into four pieces and stamped with the city arms, each fraction representing the value of a whole coin, to remedy the contraction of currency. When the King relieved the town, it was only to see his forces routed outside the walls and Cromwell's enter the gates.

Hawarden Castle, Mr. Gladstone's old residence, lies about six miles from Chester and lies back in a magnificent park about a mile from the village of Hawarden. The village is one of the prettiest and quaintest we have seen, though nearly all of it lies on one street. Nearly all of the cottages are thatched and overgrown with dog and climbing roses, while the yards are full of the most delicately tinted tea roses, roses that grow, not on bushes, but on rose trees from five to eight feet high. The New Castle, as the Gladstone residence is called, is a nineteenth-century building which came into Mr. Gladstone's possession on his marriage with Catharine Glynne, the heiress of the estate. This Miss Glynne was a direct descendant of Hugh Lupus, a cousin of William the Conqueror, who came over with the Normans and was given by William a large tract of land covering what is now known as Cheshire and Shropshire. It was this same Hugh Lupus who built the so-called "Old Castle," which forms the chief beauty of Hawarden. Of this only a splendid Norman tower, half its original height, roofless and ivy-grown, and a section of the wall that led from the keep to the living apartments, remain. The tower was built about 1075, but was repaired and restored and used as a fortress as late as 1664. This never has been out of the possession of Lupus' descendants, and was one of the strongest garrisons in the long struggle with the Welsh just across the border. The Welsh often saw fit to raid the rich plains of Cheshire, and a goodly number of troops were always kept at this garrison. My friend and I spent half of a June day in almost utter solitude at the foot of the tower. There is a sort of wall about it now that follows the line of the old moat. Generations of oaks have grown up over

the site of the living-rooms of the Norman baron. The
hill on which the tower stands is wooded from top to
base, and the solitude is so complete that the birds are
nesting in the old loop-holes of the keep. The rains
and winds of a thousand years have given the masonry
of the tower a white, clean-washed look, like the
cobble-stones of the street after a shower. One can understand, lying a morning through at the foot of the
Norman tower, why there are Maurice Hewlitts in
England. The temptation to attempt to reconstruct
the period when these things were a part of the living
fabric of the world is one that must necessarily assail
an ardent imagination. The brighter the day, the
greener the park, the more deep the significance of
their ghost of Saxon oppression, the more mystically it
speaks of "far-off, old unhappy things, and battles long
ago."

The Baron Hugh Lupus, who built this tower over-
looking the swampy forests about the Dee, built the
oldest part of the beautiful Chester Cathedral. A man
well on in years at the time of the Conquest, and having blood enough on his conscience, he determined to
found a religious house at Chester. He decided to in-
troduce the Benedictine order from France, and sent
to the great churchman St. Anselm, asking him to
come over from Rouen and organize his church and

cloister. Now, there was at Chester an old Saxon church and a very holy one, where the remains of St. Werburgh reposed. St. Werburgh was the daughter of a heathen king of the Mercians, who was buried in what is now Herefordshire. During the second Danish invasion, when the Danes were ravaging all the churches in their path, the daughter of Alfred the Great, who had devoted herself to a religious life and had founded a church at Chester, hearing that the Danes were approaching Hereford, dug up St. Werburgh's remains and, mounting her palfrey, rode over with her train to Chester. Here she reinterred St. Werburgh's remains in her own church. When St. Anselm arrived in England, he and Hugh Lupus decided upon St. Werburgh's shrine as the site for their Norman church. It was on St. Anselm's return from this mission in the west that William Rufus called him to be archbishop of Canterbury. The original Norman church was quite as large as the present cathedral, except in height. Through the twelfth, thirteenth, fourteenth, and fifteenth centuries, builders have built over and under and around the Norman church and destroyed most of it. Two sections of the original wall, with their round arches, and the bases of many of the pillars are still to be seen. These enormous pillars are not made of single stones, but of large stones fitted together with perfect symmetry into a sort of thick stone tube, the hollow center of which was filled with smaller stones and mortar. This largely explains why so little of the Norman ecclesiastical architecture is left, as the superimposed weight in time forced these composite arches apart. The building is of the soft red sandstone found all about Chester.

The cloister is perhaps the most beautiful part of the building to one who has never lived in a Catholic country. Its utter peacefulness in the afternoons I spent there, the Norman wall, with its half-effaced designs, on which the eyes of unfaith gaze in bland astonishment after a thousand years, the rain that fell so quietly or the sun that shone so remotely into the green court in the center, with its old, thick sod, its pear tree and its fleur-de-lis—they made the desirableness of the cloister in the stormy years seem not impossible. Without, Norman and Saxon butchered each other, and poachers were flayed alive, and forests planted over the ruins of freeholders' homesteads; but within the cloister the garden court was green, the ale went to the abbot's cellar and venison to his table, and though kings were slain and communities wiped out, the order of prayers and offices and penances was never broken.

. . .

Among the hundred interesting features of the cathedral, there is an old bit of English history built into the stone of the choir. In the thirteenth century, during the reign of Edward I, the monks were finishing the north side of the choir, and beautiful work they made of it, with their pointed arches of fluted stone beautifully toned by their own shadows. When King Edward came up to make war with the Welsh, he and his queen stopped at the monastery and appropriated its revenue for his campaign. Consequently, the south wall of the choir is of cheap and shallow workmanship and shabby finish, representing exactly the period of poverty the monastery endured because of the King's extremities. Further on the old rich style is resumed again.

[3]

Shropshire and
A. E. Housman

From Chester, avoiding trodden paths, Willa Cather
and her friend now make straight for Shropshire. At
once she tells her readers what has brought her there:
her faith in the verses of A. E. Housman, A Shropshire Lad. Some time still must pass, be it noted, before Housman was to attain his later reputation; but
the young woman from Nebraska is very sure of herself. It is a question of obvious excellence, permanent
worth. Confidently she commends this poetry to her
readers, a "lyric expression of great simplicity, spontaneity, and grace the like of which we have scarcely
had in the last hundred years."

In Shrewsbury, actively tracing her unknown poet, with Western enterprise she goes for further information to the files of the little country newspaper, in which many of his poems were first printed. She even telegraphs to London—and tells us so—to secure his address. This persistence, this direct attack, especially during first full days in Europe, should be noted. It is her own approach to genius.

Her later meeting with Housman, in his lodgings at Highgate, and her keen disappointment at the way in which the confrontation developed, are not dealt with in the present series. They should be mentioned, however, to complete the story. Briefly, the two young women, accompanied by Dorothy Canfield, simply went unannounced to the London address they had secured; and Housman, taken by surprise, was polite but—typically—shy and rather evasive. To the end of her life, we know, Willa Cather apparently still wanted to commit this meeting to some form, to draw conclusions, in her own mind or else on paper. It never ceased to have peculiar significance for her.

Still following the haunts of their unseen poet, the two companions now continue further, to Ludlow, in "the real Housman country." How well she describes it, the placid rivers, the cropped trees, the healing silence over all! The following year, in April Twilights,

a poem titled "Poppies on Ludlow Castle" will evoke
the mood of these hours. It is ostensibly about Sir
Philip Sidney, who had spent part of his youth there;
yet from beginning to end it is seen through Housman's eyes, even in his own meter. For the moment
Willa Cather quite naturally was Housman.

At an inn in Ludlow, "flourishing . . . before
Elizabeth came to the throne," in the chance of travel
she now first tastes the pleasure of actual dwelling in
surroundings enriched by the past. This also appeals,
immediately and powerfully. A sense of domestic in-
teriors such as only the Old World can provide is here
made a part of her awareness, if only—in later stories—
to heighten contrast with the bare and ugly houses she
knows so well in her own prairie land. She will develop
great skill in evoking old places, old settings, in a mere
sentence or two. Their amenity, ripened with time, becomes one of her permanent values; and the continued
pathetic attempts of her immigrants to transplant it
to bare country, under difficulties, becomes a favorite
theme. Often, depicting various characters who struggle with hard conditions in the New World, she makes
them recall this sweetness in the Old.

Somewhat irrelevantly, amid rather hasty writing,
Willa Cather ends her present account with an anec-
dote selected at random, one feels, from what must

have been a quantity of other possible material, probably because it was a stark tale, of betrayed love and of suicide, that appealed to her. She was ever one to look dire circumstance in the eye, with no "fussiness," as she elsewhere phrases it; and the list in her works of those who meet disaster and death is long. Indeed, the hard road of life, its penalties and punishments, and then always the inevitable end, become from the very first—once Jamesian imitation is over—her great themes.

No doubt it was this brooding meditation on ultimates that had drawn her to Housman. At this stage the young Willa Cather is herself internally diffident, feeling about life much of what he so well expressed. She is still working through a hard phase of her personal existence; when no glad cry of liberation, in secure possession of her own entity, has as yet come. So here we see another incubation at work. Like all her development, it will not be rapid. Yet once through the long tunnel of these preparatory years, when she was learning not only her craft but who she herself was, her ultimate victory will be superb.

Ludlow, July 11, 1902

THE beaten track of the summer tourist in England, from Chester to Warwick, Warwick to Stratford-on-Avon, and Stratford to London, can be soon learned and, luckily, soon avoided. Shropshire, one of the western shires which runs along the Welsh border, is the source of Mr. Housman's little volume of lyrics entitled A *Shropshire Lad.* Anyone who has ever read Housman's verse at all must certainly wish to live awhile among the hillside fields, the brookland and villages, which moved a modern singer to lyric expression of a simplicity, spontaneity, and grace the like of which we have scarcely had in the last hundred years. The remoteness, the unchangedness, and time-defying stillness of much of the Shropshire country perhaps explain Mr. Housman, as well as its own singularly individual beauty. Shrewsbury is almost the only town in the shire which is ever visited at all by foreigners. The town is almost surrounded by a loop of the Severn, which is nowhere more green and cool and clear, and nowhere more indolent and inaudible in its flowing. The broad meadows across the stream from the town are those on which Housman says that boys played football in the days of his boyhood, and as we sat beside the Severn looking across to the fields, who should come racing out over the green but a company of lads with their pigskin ball? It was in these meadows, by the way, that the boy Darwin played football and did his first botanizing when he was a pupil at the old boys' school founded in Shrewsbury by Edward VI. There is a large bronze statue of him standing now before the old school building, today used as a library. I went to Shrewsbury chiefly to get some information about Housman, and saw the old files of the little country paper where many of his lyrics first appeared as free contributions and signed "A Shropshire Lad." There was one copy of his book in the public library, but no one knew anything in particular about him. By doing some telegraphing to his London publishers, getting his London address, etc., we unintentionally created quite an excitement before we left the town, and several gentlemen, who have local reputations as being well-read to sustain, called on us to ask for the name of his publisher, etc., and were greatly astonished to hear that the book had been selling in America for six years.

It is some twenty miles south of Shrewsbury, however, that one comes upon the real Housman country

and enters the real rural Shropshire. Mr. Housman describes it as:

> In valleys of springs of rivers,
>   By Ony and Teme and Clun,
> The country for easy livers,
>   The quietest under the sun.

We arrived in Ludlow about six o'clock one afternoon, and drove through noiseless streets to our hotel.
The town is a place of some 3,500 inhabitants, somewhat smaller now than it was in Queen Elizabeth's
time. High green hills rise to the north and west, all
marked off into tiny pocket-handkerchief fields bor-
dered by green hedgerows and looking like the beds of
a large hillside garden. To the south lies the valley of
the Teme, with low, round hills on either side, none
of them wood-covered. The Teme is a narrow stream,
even for an English river, not more than twenty feet
wide anywhere, with the meadow lipping it on either
side, and the hay grass dipping into the water when the
wind is high. There are no naked, straggling clay
banks; the river does not flow through the bottom of a
ravine, but on a level with the fields, like a canal, and
it runs deep and green and clear and quiet under its
arched stone bridges. On either side of it are the pollard willows to which Mr. Abbey, the painter, so ut-

terly lost his heart when Harper Brothers sent him into rural England in his youth to make some drawings for them. They are never more than twelve feet high, with a trunk perhaps three feet thick, and little round bushy tops that make them look very much like the painted trees of the antediluvian world that are always found in toy Noah's arks. Beside this river, on the top of a cliff over a hundred feet high, rise the magnificent remains of Ludlow Castle, once one of the most important and always one of the hotly contested fortresses in the kingdom. This cliff side, from castle wall to river brink, is now sort of hanging, tipped endwise, and from rock to rock the ivy hangs powdered over with huge bouquets of blooming alder trees and climbing dog roses with stems and suckers of fabulous proportions.

There are very few modern homes at all in Ludlow. Many of the shops were shops in Queen Anne's time, and many of the more impecunious people live in houses that have been patched up since Queen Elizabeth's day. The Feathers Hotel at which we stopped was named for the Prince of Wales' crest, was a flourishing inn before Elizabeth came to the throne, and was used as a sort of overflow house for such guests as the castle could not accommodate. Almost the en-

tire interior is of black oak, with huge beams across the
ceiling, and all the windows are of tiny diamond panes.
The entire ceiling of the dining-room is carved with
the arms of various lords of the western border, and
about the great fireplace is a mass of intricate wood-
carving, culminating in the work above the mantel,
where the star of the Order of the Garter and its cred-
itable motto are cut the size of a tea-table top. My
sleeping-room overhangs the street, and I walk up an
inclined plane from the dresser to my bed, but, for all
that, I never expect to sleep again in a place so beautiful. The knocker on the spike-studded outer door alone
would make a house desirable. No one comes here except the country gentlemen about, when they ride into
town, or folk who bicycle over from the neighbouring
towns of a Sunday. The only other guests beside ourselves who seem established here are a theatrical couple from London, who are spending their honeymoon
here, and, as they are desirous of solitude, we never en-
ounter them except at meals or occasionally in some
willow thicket along the river where they have embow-
ered themselves. A bicycling pair from Chicago came
in the other day, propped their Baedeker against the
water bottle at dinner, read it madly aloud, then de-
parted, with a little whir and a little cloud of dust, into
the quiet of the Teme and the misty hills that is never

broken except by the chimes that ring the quarter hours so melodiously one is glad to have them pass, and, three times a day, play the whole of some old English air. I heard a chime, at Evesham, which played the whole of "Drink to Me Only with Thine Eyes" more rhythmically than anyone but Bispham can sing it, and played it always in the most unusual and uncanny hours, when the whole performance seemed supernatural.

Mr. Housman is by no means the only singing Shropshire lad; Sir Philip Sidney courted the lyric muse there long before him. Ludlow Castle was magnificently renewed and enlarged by Sir Henry Sidney, his father, who was made Governor of the Border under Elizabeth, and Philip spent the formative part of his boyhood and youth in that country, which is surely the country for the making of poets if ever one was. The ruins of the great hall built by Sir Henry for the council of the governing heads of Wales, and of the extensive chambers and banqueting-halls built for the entertainment of his royal sovereign and her peers, tax the imagination; they so far surpass modern notions of splendour. The most interesting part of the castle, however, is the keep itself, which was built by Joce de Dinan, a Norman knight, who also built the circu-

lar chapel, dedicated to St. Mary Magdalene, which is
the only one of its kind left standing in England. The
castle and its lords played an exceedingly prominent
part in the Wars of the Roses, as it was the place of
residence of Richard Plantagenet, Duke of York; and
the two sons of Edward IV, who were afterward mur-
dered in the tower, were reared and educated there.
Their two adjoining rooms, with their little fireplaces,
are still pointed out. There Prince Arthur, son of
Henry VII, died, leaving his wife an inheritance to his
brother Henry VIII. But the prettiest chapter of the
castle's long history is an early one, dating back to the
day of its Norman founder, Joce de Dinan, which is
beautifully told by a fourteenth-century chronicler.
Joce de Dinan had a mortal foe, Walter de Lacy, who
was also a stalwart knight, and one morning, in a com-
bat which took place by the river below the castle,
de Lacy and two of his companions were taken pris-
oner and confined in the keep. They were well treated
and permitted to dine with the household, and one of
de Lacy's knights, an Arnold de Lisle, won the affection of a little French maiden, Marion de la Bruyère,
who was being reared in Joce de Dinan's household.
She effected his escape by tying sheets and towels together, and his lord escaped with him. Some nine
months afterward Joce de Dinan went away to marry

his daughter to a young lord, and left the castle in charge of fifty knights, going himself secretly. Poor Marion, who had not seen her lover since the day of his escape, and who was by this time well-nigh desperate for loneliness, sent a message and a rope ladder to Arnold, telling him the weak state of the garrison in order to persuade him to come to her. He came, and went with her to her apartments in the unguarded side of the castle that was protected by the precipice, but after him came a hundred armed knights up the ladder, and they slew the garrison in their beds and put to the sword every vassal of de Dinan, every man, woman, and child in the town nestled below the castle. When Marion of the Heath arose next morning, she opened her windows and saw the smoke of the burning village, and dead men lying by the wall. She caught up her lover's sword and ran it through his breast, and threw herself from her window down the side of the cliff that is now so white with dog roses and alder bloom.

[4]

The Canals of England

The untraveled young woman from the Divide progresses further. As with all Americans fresh to England, as she travels her attention is drawn to the "tiny locomotives, with their faint, indignant, tiny whistle." She is evidently contrasting them, as she writes, with the trains that had been so much a part of her childhood in Red Cloud, those great engines with another scream, as she elsewhere defines it, a "world-wide call for men."

Her observation is next engaged, absorbed, by what at the outset may seem the most unlikely of subjects: English canals, placid and narrow, winding peacefully, "obsequiously" even, through the quiet countryside. Having stumbled upon them by chance, from Chester onward she simply follows her interest. We can fairly see her at work, as a young journalist, asking strings of questions, avid for information about the curious barges, the whole existence of the men and women who live on them. Factually she takes it all in, putting it here to paper. This is a new and unexpected subject, quite to her taste.

"This peculiar sect of people" she sees to be the highly individual types they are. The women, especially, fascinate her. While their husbands follow the towpath, they manage the tiller. They tend their children, and do the housekeeping, set for life upon these narrow craft.

Our young observer follows her lead; she explores their cabins, notes the furnishings, the short sleeping-berths. She appraises their cleanliness, comments upon the discomfort. In a score of ways she imaginatively sinks herself into the whole course of their lives, reconstructing the cycle, for both men and women, born and bred, living and dying, in small cabins here on a tame canal. Intimate habits and pleasures, family quarrels—nothing escapes her. She proceeds with gusto, following the typical boatman even to "the end of his run."

She is aware that "neither the consolation of education nor religion"—mark the phrase, for here early it includes all her highest values—is granted them at the end; and she does not shrink from presenting a candid picture. Once she has discovered the canal folk on her first evening in Chester, she follows them, alive with curiosity, even—as she puts it—to the "glitter of things untried," to London itself.

What was retained from all this unexpected, highly individual interest? We have here, apparently, at least part of the genesis of a whole type of woman, quite unknown to Edwardian fiction, who will appear early in Willa Cather's writing and then never altogether leave it. This woman challenged her imagination, "teased" it, to use Sarah Orne Jewett's word, persistently for years. She is ample and heroic, rather than refined and delicate. Capable, free, with spontaneous manners, inured to hardship—she is a woman generously built, adequate to all the burdens of a hard life. Whatever may be her destiny, she is a match for it. Quite possibly, she may represent one ideal of Willa Cather for herself.

Once defined, we shall find her again and again, in one variant or another. She first appears in full scale as Alexandra in O Pioneers! of 1913; then both as Thea and as her capable mother in The Song of the Lark, two years later. As My Ántonia, in 1918, the type grows to its greatest beauty, reaching fulfillment; although as late as 1932 she will appear once more as the loyal country wife of gentle city-bred "Neighbour Rosicky," of the story by that name in Obscure Destinies.

All these women—and others—are recognizable sisters of the strange free creatures discovered one evening, unexpectedly, here on a placid English canal. Far beyond Willa Cather's conscious imaginings at this early time, therefore, we can here trace important creation to come. A new type of "strong" woman, completely different from the heroines of contemporary fiction, but with obvious resemblances to familiar figures in various pioneering communities back in Nebraska, is stumbled upon in the chances of travel. Once seen, she immediately becomes of high interest; and, once apprehended, she will remain an impressive type, in stories at this time a full generation ahead. Thus proceeds the mysterious development of creative power, foreshadowing even the still distant future.

London, July 16, 1902

EVERY American travelling in England gets his own individual sport out of the toy passenger and freight trains and the tiny locomotives, with their faint, indignant, tiny whistle. Especially in western

England one wonders how the business of a nation can possibly be carried on by means so insufficient. The one great canal in the west answers this question and largely takes the place of the freight car, affording a circuitous but continuous passage from Liverpool to London. From the Mersey River, which forms the Liverpool harbor, the canal runs west to Chester, a distance of about fifteen miles, then forty-five miles southwest to Shrewsbury, then east to Birmingham, and from there southeast to London.

This canal, which is owned by several companies and called by several names, is altogether different from an American canal; it is in every way smaller, quieter, less obtrusive, seemingly not to be greatly depended upon, but in reality quite as reliable as anything we have. It is nowhere more than thirty feet wide, and winds so obsequiously among the green meadows that but for the hedge beside the towpath one might lose it altogether. The boats are of two builds; the largest are about seventy-five feet long and fifteen wide and carry a cargo of about fifty tons. These are called barges or bachelor boats, and are manned by a crew of four men, no women being allowed in the crew. They carry grain, pig iron, wrought iron, and heavy or bulky freight. I saw one loaded to the water edge with bridge frames from the United States Steel company. These boats are drawn by a single horse only, but always a draft horse of powerful build. These larger ones are the only boats on the canal that are taken to Liverpool to be loaded. They are taken into the great ship canal at Elsmere Port, and some fourteen of them are hitched to a tug, and dragged through the heavy swell of the Mersey, which almost buries them entirely, to the Liverpool harbour.

The larger are greatly outnumbered by the smaller and lighter "flats." These boats are as long as the barges, but are of lighter build and nowhere more than five feet wide, their capacity being only thirty tons. They are loaded so heavily that they just avoid dipping water, though the canal is as still as only stagnant water can be. These boats receive their cargo at Elsmere Port, as they would immediately be overturned in the impetuous tides that sweep up the Mersey. Neither barges nor flats have even a pretense of a deck. The cabin is a sort of dugout, exactly five by six, and the remaining space in the boat is every inch of it given up to the freight, which is stowed in from the top, very much as it would be in a rowboat. When the cargo is once in place, heavy sheets of oilcloth are drawn over it and tied down. While this method of stowing and protecting a cargo from the weather may look insecure to a landsman, every sort of merchandise, from perfumes and fruit to upright pianos, is shipped thus.

These narrow boats, of which there are nearly three thousand now running on the canal, are responsible for a peculiar sect of people, an element in the British working classes little heard of outside of England. If Darwin had wished to study further the part played by environment in the differentiation of species, he could have taken no better subjects than the canal people. Originally the boatmen were Englishmen, with all the earmarks of the British workingman. They have become a solitary and peculiar people who have not their like in the world—Englishmen only in their speech. The canal boatman is a sort of half-land, half-water gypsy, a vagabond who manages to keep within the trace of labour, a tramp of one road, the best-paid and worst-nourished manual labourer in the kingdom.

In the stern of each flat there is a cave-like cabin, five by six, and in this cabin live, winter and summer, the boatman, his wife, and anywhere from two to ten children. One of the managers of the Chester division of the canal told me that it had scarcely ever occurred in his time that the son of a boatman had followed any other than his father's calling. The shackles of caste were never more adamantine among the Hindoos than these people have made them for themselves. The men invariably wear the same cap and corduroy trousers, and the women are never seen without their peculiar headdress, which is seen nowhere else in England, but which closely resembles that of the women in some parts of Italy. These women are quite as good boatmen as their husbands, and take the more difficult of the two principal tasks, managing the tiller while their husbands follow the towpaths. The woman does this, too, with half a dozen children clinging to her skirts. In addition to managing the tiller and tending the children, she does what housekeeping can be done in a box six feet by five and just high enough to stand in. In this cave there is a stove, a table on hinges, and a berth which is let down from the wall, in which the boatman and his wife sleep. The berth is too short to admit of their lying straight, but the boatwomen assured us that it was quite comfortable to sleep doubled up when you got used to it. The boatwoman seldom carries a change of clothes, and neither she nor her husband undress when they go to bed at night, but kick off their shoes, wearing their clothing as faithfully as an animal does his fur. The managers of the company insist on a certain show of cleanliness, and the walls and floors of the cabin are usually scrubbed until they are white as wax. Both the men and women have a passion for brass; they stud the walls of the cabin with brass-headed tacks and collect brass cooking utensils and candlesticks greedily.

My interest in the canal was aroused the first night we spent in Chester. A number of flats were tied up at the lock house waiting to be lowered to the level, sandy plains about the river Dee. In the course of a walk we came accidentally upon that part of the canal which runs under the Northgate street bridge, at the bottom of a cut seventy-five feet deep in the solid rock. The cut is narrow, and on either side the red sandstone walls rise sheer, loops of wild vines hanging from the crevices, yellow sweet clover growing here and there, and the tops of both cliffs overhung by that species of tall, bushy alder tree, white with bloom, that makes English gardens so beautiful in early summer. At the foot of these red cliffs, in the green-black water that reflected the walled gardens high above it, we saw these long gondolas of trade, with those brown, foreign-looking men and women eating their dinner on top of the dugout cabin. The lock-keeper afterward told me that the cut had often been painted and sold as "A Quiet Waterway, Venice." When the canal people had finished their dinner and rinsed the dishes off in the canal, the men struck off for the public house and their women began to dress to go into town to wit-

ness the coronation festivities, which came off, coronation or no. They dressed in the open air, in the vestibule to their cabin, probably because it was cooler
there than in the cabin itself. Our gaze disconcerted
them not at all; their backs and breasts and arms were
as brown as the darkest Neapolitan's. The woman
nearest me, when she had made her toilet, dressed her
little boy in his first trousers, which she had made on
board for him, and when he whined to have his hands
in his pockets she threatened to put his petticoats back
on him, quite in the fashion of decent, land-staying
mothers, though the lock-keeper said she would be as
tipsy as a soldier when she got back. Like all the boatwomen, this woman had been born in the cabin of a
flat, had been a baby and had all her childish ailments
and grown to maidenhood shut in a box five by six,
with half a dozen brothers and sisters. She had been
courted and married somewhere between the tiller and
the towpath, tied up at Chester or Birmingham, and
spent the night at a public house by way of a honeymoon, and borne her children in the cabin where she
herself was born. But the canal boatwoman certainly
does not consider herself unfortunate. She is fond of
her children, but the fact that they clamber all over
the top of the boat like monkeys, and nimbly jump
from stern ashore to gather buttercups, never alarms

her. She had the same dangerous playground. "If they lose their holt, they kin ketch by their toes," she remarks. When the children are a little older they will do practically all the work, and she and "him," as she calls her husband, can lie all day on top of the hot oilcloth that covers the cargo, and smoke their pipes or quarrel over their bottle, as they feel disposed. The boatwoman likes to get pleasantly tipsy and lie without any feeling of responsibility and watch the green fields and little towns go by, and she can do this as soon as the children are old enough to be pressed into service. That is her season of roses. But when her boys have learned to manage a boat well—that is to say, when they are about eighteen years of age—they marry some boatman's daughter and take the management of a boat of their own. There is never any question about a son's getting his own boat: no man who was not born on one of these frail, cramped crafts can ever manage or live on them, and the demand for boatmen grows every day. As soon as her daughters are fifteen, some boatman's lad hurries them into marriage. When a boy gets a boat of his own, he must have a wife to avoid wasting his earnings on a hired helper. Only a boatman's daughter can help him at his work and endure the hardships of his life. When he takes his wife to his new boat, a trail of boats follow him through the night, singing and carrying lanterns hung on poles. This is his wedding march. When he dies they lay him out in his cabin, shut the door and tie a black rag on it, carry him to the end of his run, where they bury him. It is not exactly his native earth, for he was born in a cabin, but is the part of the earth with which he was most nearly connected; the place where he tied up at night, and where he found his favourite public house; in short, literally and metaphorically, it is the end of his run.

When the sons and daughters are all married, the boatman and his wife must take up the management of the boat again, when they are old and stiff and given to drink. These old couples were the only discontented people I saw on the canal. They have neither the consolation of education nor religion. Not one in a hundred can read, and they are the most frank and unabashed of pagans. The old lock-keeper at Chester had several long talks with me about the extent of his responsibility for their poor souls. To use his words, spoken with the deepest and most sincere melancholy, "They won't listen to the Bible, howsoever I try 'em. They don't fear an awful God, much less trust a loving Saviour." The lock-keeper, a very thin, pale man and a Covenanter, cannot speak of this aspect of the boatman's life without deep emotion. He spends a great deal of time silent in the sunshine on the lockhouse porch, his eyes closed, but not asleep, and I am inclined to believe that he is often praying. He has his worldly ambition as well, and it seems a queer one enough. One morning when he was clipping his hedge he told me that he saved a little money each year to one end: after he got his eight daughters married off, and his wife comfortably settled for old age, then his turn was to come, and he was going to imagine himself "a young lad again, mayhap," and start off with reverential awe to see—Niagara Falls! "The mightiest revelation of the Almighty left us now-a-days, as I take it."

But, unlettered as they are, the boatmen are apt enough at getting what they want out of life. The finer aspects of their peculiar culture have puzzled the government detectives for years. The boats carry a great deal of liquor, and the lock-keeper explained to me that the boatman loads on his cargo at the bonded warehouse, taking with it a sample of the same liquor, the bottle shut in a glass case and sealed with a long inscription stamped into the wax. On the trip the boatman can take seven buckets full of whisky out of each barrel and yet deliver it stronger than the sample. The cleverest detectives have never yet found their means of adulteration.

The old lock-keeper, being a man of conscience and reflection and "having daughters of his own," grieves a good deal over some of the uglier aspects of the life of the barge girls. He said he had got good places for them and prevailed upon them to go out to service time and again, but they can not endure either steady work or indoor life. The girl always runs away to marry the boatman's lad, who beat her with his fist when she was a little girl and who will beat her with his fists again, and her children after her. No more will the boatman quit his boat. He has been a gypsy from his cradle. He follows his mule and smokes his pipe, winding through fields and woods, a pagan, letterless, lawless, godless, who tramps up and down through the heart of England, yet mingles not with Englishmen. "The road to perdition," the lock-keeper called the towpath, but it is surely the fairest road that ever went there, though we hear tell that many of them are fair. It is a path that runs by shadowed woods and the sweetest hay fields in the world, that is sown with buttercups and scarlet poppies, that is skirted by hedges and runs neighbourly with full, quiet rivers. We began our acquaintance with the canal at Chester and tested the towpath, we found it again at Shrewsbury, crossed and recrossed it on the way to Birmingham, followed it through the Avon country, slept near it at Evesham; and when we were running into London—a wilderness of bigness and newness and strangeness— between the bulk of warehouses, from the maze of streets, emerged the canal, a part of the countryside lost in London, and we welcomed it like the homely and trustworthy face of an old friend, good to see in this glitter of things untried.

[5]

London: The East End

This is the least well-balanced, certainly the most compulsive and strongly written article of the present series. It transmits a major shock, Willa Cather's continuing encounter with a depressed world that previously—it becomes obvious—she had never thought much about. It also reflects a discomfort so acute as at times to verge on torture, wrung from a provincial American girl now plunged into the dregs, the off-scourings, of metropolitan existence.

Typically, in London she seeks lodging in the City, far from the more conventional West End. She has, though, chosen a very sordid neighborhood, and here we promptly find her intimately confronted, fascinated and repelled at the same time, by the foul impact. She had apparently anticipated only that a part of town like this would be convenient for independent sight-seeing: it was of course near to the Tower, to the Guildhall, Saint Paul's. Yet the actuality, about her on every street, proved overwhelming. All she could achieve at first, she tells us candidly, was a mere "watching the procession with perplexity."

One realizes that Willa Cather had, after all, been brought up in cleanliness, with abundant air, light, and sun about her. This spreading depravity, this foulness under soiled skies, these swarming, dirty, rowdy people were unlike anything she had ever imagined. The shambling, filthy crowds, the shameless topers in the public houses, the gin-soaked slatterns; she contemplates them day and night. On High Holborn, in the Strand, on the Embankment, everywhere she traces the misery, the degradation! From the beginning, here in London, it is human problems and not the tourist's coverage that have become important.

A full quarter of a century later the horror of this inhumanity is still burning within her! In the short story already mentioned, "Neighbour Rosicky," published in Obscure Destinies in 1932 but dating from 1928, she puts into her immigrant farmer's mouth sentences of moving gratitude for his escape from crowded Cheapside and grinding sweatshop poverty there—to sweet and open country once more, to Nebraska. Across the years, the slums of 1902 are evoked in detail; and every sentence redraws the original picture.

Next she turns her attention to the street-bred shop girls; and although she acknowledges at once the good qualities of the conventional ones, in or about Bond Street, what holds her is not such comparatively tame destinies, but those of their poorer sisters, the shoddy, often drunken, raucous, and dirty human flesh, existing somehow below all of her previous standards.

All this went deep, even to incoherence. Some of it we can trace, the following year, in a poem titled "London Roses," on the flower-sellers, in her April Twilights. It bears enigmatic marks of powerful, unresolved, and unexplained emotion; and, obscure though it is, Willa Cather did retain it in a later revised edition of this book, although others—including two of travel, on Paris and Montmartre—were discarded.

We catch arresting further glimpses of her, during these days in London, in the gallery at the opera or one of the theaters, overhearing conversations, observing, watching. Here also was human material that clamored for absorption. One suspects that to her, even from the beginning, the Ántonias of this world—whether in a great city, or out on the wind-swept prairie—were always more valuable than the superior women she here looks down on in the boxes. These last are mentioned rather indifferently. She will accord that they are "very well bred and often remarkably beautiful"; but she seems not tempted to give them much further notice.

Then, still following the single thread of her personal interest, she again shifts, this time to a quite local scene, a religious procession in London's Italian colony. Quite possibly, we must realize, on that very day she might have been an onlooker at some splendid service, perhaps at the Abbey, in Westminster. Instead, we find her in a poor street, standing in the rain, reverently watching dignified old women, or pale younger ones, or dark-polled little Italian children pass by.

She feels her kinship with these people; not with the dreadful creatures, also watching, beyond the police lines. Here is her world, her scale of values. Under leaden skies, the attempt of these poor Italians to decorate their little shrines, to make some show of beauty and color even in "the heathen heart of the London slums," these obviously draw her affection and loyalty.

Valuing this humanity, this variety of religion, in contrast with what surrounded it, we can see how she is already predisposed in sentiment to a Latin, even a Catholic, way of life. We know, further, how this motif will develop, over a whole career, into accounts of simple faith under hard conditions, in New Mexico or French Canada. Yet in 1902, of course, all this was far in the future.

She has thought of what Kipling had to say. Now she remembers Hogarth, and with what skill he had in his time fixed these "hideous distortions of a night-mare." So we find her looking another grim aspect of reality in the face; questioning, so to speak, a further sphinx barring the road. In the grim vastness of great London, she has unerringly found the people who in-terest her. None of them are the elite; far from it. Here, as always, her world is the large, vibrant, palpi-tating one of ordinary people. Nor is she apologetic for what holds her.

London, July 22, 1902

W HEN I came to London two weeks ago my first endeavour was to avoid that part of the city given over to pensions and lodging-houses, and to make it pos-sible to live in a part of the city near Russell and Meck-lenberg squares or about the British Museum. We managed to find a very comfortable and satisfactory little hotel, patronized chiefly by folk from the country who come to town to do their modest shopping, on King Street, off Cheapside. That put us within two squares of the Bank of England and the Lord Mayor's residence, almost under the dome of St. Paul's, and on the same street up which Lady Jane Grey daily went to meet her judges at the Guildhall. The Lord Mayor still goes up to the Guildhall by the same street, and he drives by our windows daily in scarlet and gold. This is rather the bargain-counter end of London; by no means extreme, like the Whitechapel section, but the part of the town where one is always among the common people: small tradesmen, shop girls, clerks, people who go a-shopping with slender purses, young men who aspire to be men of fashion on small salaries. We came here because we wished to be in the heart of the old city of London, within walking distance of the Tower, Old Bailey, and the Temple; but the living city and not the dead one has kept us here, and the hard, garish, ugly mask of the immediate present drags one's attention quite away from the long past it covers. One starts out at ten o'clock, before which hour of the day no shops or buildings are open, to make pilgrimages in the orthodox fashion; but one ends by merely watching the procession with perplexity. If the street life, not the Whitechapel street life, but that of the common but so-called respectable part of the town, is in any city more gloomy, more ugly, more grimy, more cruel than in London, I certainly don't care to see it. Sometimes it occurs to one that possibly all the failures of this generation, the world over, have been suddenly swept into London, for the streets are a restless, breathing, malodorous pageant of the seedy of all nations.

But of all the shoddy foreigners one encounters, there are none so depressing as the London shoddy. We have spent morning after morning on High Holborn or the Strand, watching this never-ending procession of men in top hats, shabby boots, ragged collars; they invariably have a flower in their buttonhole, a briar pipe between their teeth, and an out-of-the-fight look in the eyes that ranges anywhere from utter listlessness to sullen defiance. Stop at any corner on the Strand at noon and you will see a bar, the street doors wide open, and a crowd of labouring men, red-faced and wet-eyed, pouring can after can of liquor down their throats. Usually there are several old women whining and complaining and tugging at their man's arm, but if one gets her husband's pewter pot away from him she usually finishes it herself with evident satisfaction. One cannot come to realize at once what an absolutely gin-soaked people these London working-folk are. Time and again we have seen sturdy, bonny, well-dressed little children trying with the most touching seriousness and gentleness to steer home two parents, both of whom were so far gone in their cups that the little folk had great ado to keep them on their feet at all. A drunken man, fairly well clad and looking the prosperous workman, will walk down the street, his hands in his pockets, beside his wife who carries the baby, cursing her with a richness and variety of phrase leaving one breathless, and no one pays the least attention to him. When I am on the street at night in this part of the town, I am always perfectly sure that men are mauling women with their fists or battering them up with furniture just around the corner anywhere. I am no voice of an oppressed sex crying aloud, however; the women drink their share. Yesterday, passing through St. James's Park in the rain, I counted the women lying shelterless, flat on the ground, in poses which passed belief, dead to the world. The park benches are always full of them. The beautiful river front on the east side of the Thames called the Albert Embankment, from which one gets the most satisfying and altogether happy view of the Houses of Parliament up the river, is night and day thronged with drunken, homeless men and women who alternately claw each other with their nails and give each other a chew of tobacco.

At night the high white globular lights which flank this marble terrace are beautifully reflected in the river, and by each light post hangs a life-preserver to re-call any tipsy wretch who may drop over the wall to end his useful activities. But very few of these night birds are fond of water, and next to gin they are enam-oured of life; of these muddy day skies and leaky night skies, of their own bench along the Embankment, of the favourite neighbour they beat or chew or claw, of the sting of cheap gin in empty stomachs, and the ex-citing game of chess they play with the police back and forth across those marble squares.

About the London shop girls of the meaner sort no derogatory remarks can be too strong, just as no com-mendation can be too high of the courtesy, honesty, and good nature of the girls who wait on you in the shops on Oxford and Bond streets. This court-born, alley-nursed, street-bred girl is everywhere. Sometimes she is sober, oftener she is not. She sells you flowers and fruit on every corner, serves in bars and cheap eat-ing-houses. We have nothing at all at home to corre-spond to her. Her voice is harder than her gin-sodden face, it cuts you like a whiplash as she shouts, "Rowses! rowses! penny a bunch," or "All the words of the h'Opry!" When she is sober she sleeps under cover somewhere; when she isn't she sleeps on the steps of the Nelson column in Trafalgar and likes that quite as well.

The shop girl who rather prides herself on being respectable, and sleeping under a roof, and maybe going to church, is in a class of her own. Her round boy's straw hat, her wonderful coat, her lace and cheap jewellery, her stooped shoulders, untidy hair, and "I-can-take-care-of-myself-sir" air make her easily recognizable. She has absolutely nothing of the neatness and trimness which characterize our working girls at home. She would blush to wear a gingham shirtwaist, preferring rather to feel elegant in a cotton satin one of unspeakable griminess. She wears flowers and paste jewels, but she seldom bathes, never has enough hairpins, and considers toothbrushes necessary only for members of the royal family.

The most advantageous place to see her is in the gallery at Covent Garden or one of the better theatres, when she has come out with one of her chums with the purpose of being both elegant and intellectual. She has her hair curled all over her head, is always rouged and heavily powdered, and she scans the house with her glasses, pointing out to her friends the nobility in the boxes. She affirms that her second cousin is a friend of the chiropodist of this duchess, and the history she proceeds to paint for the very well-bred and often remarkably beautiful woman at whom she points is beyond the dreams of Edna Southworth. When she has finished with the dukes and duchesses she begins on the opera company. Her scandals have infinite variety and the detail of a past master in realism, and I must admit that I envy her her fecundity of invention. One of the favourite relaxations of the flower girl—that name that we have been taught to associate with idyllic innocence—is fisticuffing her friends and acquaintances. She is by turns fury and bacchante, and a cruel sight it is to behold her leaping through the streets in the impetus of her gin-fed joy. Whoever thinks that Kipling exaggerated conditions in his "Record of Badalia Herodsfoot," let him come and see. Since I have been in London I have thought Kipling a greater man than I ever thought him before. Coming to the city fresh from the colonies, he caught with admirable truth the colouring of the place, together with its greatness and griminess.

On Sunday last the Italians of London, who are both fewer and poorer than those of New York, celebrated the feast of Our Lady of Mount Carmel. As Miss Dorothy Canfield had joined us and is particularly interested in all phases of Italian life at home and abroad, we went into the Italian quarters to see the procession. It was a most unfortunate day for anything that required enthusiasm. The skies were an even, ashen grey, hopeless and changeless, the rain descended lightly but steadily. The streets were a thick, gritty paste of mud. Where the poor southerners found courage to erect and decorate the arch at the head of the street, I could not conjecture. There was scarcely a window that had not a little shrine before it, with a tiny image and burning candles, carefully protected from the rain. The Italian quarter here is a poor place enough, and these attempts at ceremonial splendour in spite of time, absence, poverty, and distance, in spite of the oppressive greyness, in spite of the oppressively ugly city, were not a little pathetic. The lace curtains were tacked to the brick walls outside the windows, and, poor as the people are, nearly every window had a garland or bunch of cut flowers. The approach of the festal procession was announced by a slow march played by drums and fifes that had, on this occasion, no military suggestion whatever. The air was intensely appealing and individual, though it recalled a little some parts of *Cavalleria Rusticana*. First came the guards, then the thurifer, cross-bearer, and acolytes, glorious spots of colour in the grey English drip. Then came men of various religious societies in costume, all with bowed heads, praying devoutly, never heeding that their gorgeous apparel was trailing in the mud. Then more thurifers and acolytes and clergy and holy images, then women, bareheaded and praying, then a body of Italian boys, all in red surplices, their little shiny black heads bowed and their hands clasped together.

Some of the older girls who marched in the line seemed quite pale from emotion. The old women were simply dignified and melancholy. So far from being a street show, the procession was a religious ceremony, even to me, who understood neither its origin nor significance. Before one realized it one was all clouded about with mysticism as with incense; fire of some sort burned in one, enthusiasm none the less real that one had little idea what it was for. These poor Latins, undauntedly trying to carry a little of the light and colour and sweet devoutness of a Latin land into their grey, cold London had done with us what a great actor can sometimes do. I did not see one self-conscious looking figure in all the procession. Never did a little boy smile or poke his neighbour. The tiniest child was able to abandon itself wholly to this beautiful experience they made for themselves in the heathen heart of the London slums. The police stood in double file along the streets to protect the worshippers from what stood without, and what stood without I know, for I stood among them; Gomorrah stood without, and Sodom, Babylon shorn of both splendour and power; the howling, hooting, heathen London mobs; men drunk, women drunk, unwashed and unregenerate. I stood next a man in a top hat, with a frock coat buttoned up over his undershirt. Next him stood a girl with a straw hat and a heavy cloak, under which she wore no dress waist. This cloak was finished in a piece of dirty cat fur. She had white lips and few teeth, and her face was covered with eruptions. She could hardly have been twenty. There was Gin Moll and Barley Sally, their old bonnets tilted like horns over their bleary eyes, their skirts on wrong-side-first. They stared at the far distance and swore quietly. The thrifty coster boys sold standing room on top of their barrows. These people who have never been inside a church, this sodden heathendom, made the setting of the devout little procession as it moved slowly along. Said Kipling: "A city where the common people are without religion and without God, but are nightly drunken and howl in the streets like jackals, the men and the women together." * Of all the British painters, surely Hogarth

---

* Miss Cather was obviously quoting from memory. Kipling's text, with a few minor changes, is to be found in "One View of the Question," in his volume *Many Inventions*.

was the only realist and the only man who knew his London. Lower London today is exactly what it was when he studied and hated it. Every day, faces from "The Idle Apprentice," "Cruelty," and "The Harlot's Progress" pass one in the streets like the hideous distortions of a nightmare.

[6]

London: Burne-Jones's Studio

In the previous article Willa Cather has dwelt long and insistently on the most sordid sides of London poverty. Now, changing to another interest, contemporary English painting—in which she appears not only as well grounded, but even anxious to deliver herself of strongly held theories—she will guide us to the "beautiful surfaces" of the metropolis, to the West End and beyond.

Nowhere is her awareness of the peculiar quality of place, her hypersensitiveness to whole regions of light and color, better shown than as she accomplishes this transition. We are given a chromatic ascension from murky depths, passing from drabness through a transitional zone of "splendid grey," to the wholly different palette of another part of town. She is quick to fix the particular colors of all the growing things, which, as always, she takes time to enumerate.

The solid "non-communicative" houses of Kensington draw her notice; as a good recording instrument, she sets herself to express their peculiarly British effects. Then through a high brick wall she introduces us into Sir Edward Burne-Jones's studio. Because of her admiration for his pictures this setting had for her reality.

She finds the place in charge of a certain "James, valet to Sir Edward's person and to his art," who in his knowing ignorance and cockney loyalty has drawn her attention; and she makes for us quite a little portrait of him. So it is with no great surprise that we find the entrance lodge, the "bare tank" of the studio itself, and, above all, this active-minded, talkative guardian—even with his own name—eventually reappearing in further work. Only very lightly disguised, they enter an early short story, titled "The Marriage of Phædra," collected in The Troll Garden, of 1905. Even James's pipe and his Sporting Life, as we see them here, are retained.

An unfinished picture by Burne-Jones, on the studio

wall, also grows in importance. Willa Cather medi-
tates how "the realization of it must have caused him
not a few low moments," no doubt comparing them
with similar difficulties of her own. This same unfinished canvas—with another subject invented for it, to
be sure—will finally provide even a title for her story.

Following this interest, Willa Cather now goes to
every studio, apparently, accessible to her in London.
She mentions both Watts's and Rossetti's, and further
—seriously—"that house beautiful of Egyptian wood-
work and Moorish tiles and priceless stone-work and
glass-work from the Orient": Sir Frederick Leighton's.
How completely this description recalls for us the high
"artistic" taste of 1902!

There is more than an echo of it, I believe, in the
setting for another Troll Garden story, that concerning
"Flavia and Her Artists." In the smoking-room of its
"House of Song," created by a rich and ambitious
American woman as a similar setting, we find walls
adorned studio fashion with "pipes and curious weap-
ons"; while the firelight throws "an orange glow on the
Turkish hangings." We are told, indeed: "There was
about the darkened room some suggestion of certain
chambers in the Arabian Nights, opening on a court of
palms"—not at all unlike the "shadowy Arabian hall"

with the "high-walled orchard" described in this article.

Apart from a small but serious curtain lecture on the advanced æsthetic theories of the day, this is all that Willa Cather has to tell us, this summer, about the art of painting. Yet we can, I believe, here trace typical steps in her process of assimilation. As always, she goes immediately toward her own interest, with vigor. Here it was Burne-Jones's style that had first attracted her. While this mood lasts, adjacent fields might lie completely neglected, even permanently. Next she must silently integrate her own reality, what she had discovered at first hand with what she had expected to find. On this first journey to Europe there were bound to be major surprises; some radical accommodation to the unexpected must often have been necessary. Finally, after "filtering" it all "slowly through the blood" —to use the phrase she got from Stephen Crane—she contrives her grand design, something her own, of power and permanence.

Painting, as here, was for her at first perhaps even the major art. It did not remain so, although it took a while for this fact to become clear. Meanwhile, she also made use of sculpture to strike a lyric note; and the short story titled "The Sculptor's Funeral," also in The Troll Garden, is a record of this—unique—attempt.

Architecture she ever deeply enjoyed, and she uses it, as the years go by, always more capably. Yet she never tries the portrait of an architect as artist.

It is music, finally, that she will make her vehicle, especially in her full-length novels. And it is through three short stories, "The Garden Lodge," " 'A Death in the Desert,' " and "A Wagner Matinée," all also in The Troll Garden, that she seems finally to have come to her decision.

There is good reason for it. After extended experiment it seems to have become clear to Willa Cather that for the purposes she had in mind, music had the highest evocative power, especially music combined with drama—that is, opera. She found that she could more effectively describe on paper how one was moved by a song or an aria to mark the development in some splendid plot, than by a canvas or a bas-relief.

Retrospectively, these studio visits on her first journey to London thus provide interesting insight. She finds good material among the painters, it is true, and learns how to make use of it. Yet, once experiments have been made, and their results appraised, for the enhancing values of "art," in her fiction, she goes off in another direction.

THE beautiful surfaces and the beautiful life of London lie from Trafalgar Square westward through St. James's Park and Hyde Park, along Piccadilly, through Kensington to Hammersmith. From Trafalgar westward the very colour of the city changes; the grimy blackness of the smoke-laden town grows to a splendid grey about the National Gallery and St. Martin-in-the-Fields, and from there the colour runs gradually into a higher and higher key, into the glorious green of the parks and the bold white of the club houses along Piccadilly, and finally into the broad asphalts of Kensington that are covered, or rather dusted, with a yellow sand that catches the sunlight like gold powder, lying bright between their lines of elm and plane trees. On those rare occasions when there is sunshine in London, it seems all to be concentrated along the winding avenues of Kensington, where it plays bravely upon the endless rows of high, white, cement-faced houses, and the high garden walls whose dull brick is crowned by iron lattice-work through which one sees the beautiful sanded gardens, yellow and smooth, without a blade of grass, but with beds of scarlet and crimson geraniums and orange nas-

turtiums, gaudier than Browning's "gaudy melon
flower," set close together as though someone had
spilled a pot of paint on the sand. About the edges of
these little gay Saharas grow tall hawthorn bushes, and
the variegated laurel, with brilliant white patches all
over its glossy leaves, and lilacs that droop indolently
over the wall, and stiff, hardy holly, green and variegated, and the polled locusts, cut round and thick into
balls of yellow-green, just the shape of the pollard willows. Behind these gardens are the dull brick houses,
never painted, and keeping the natural colour of the
brick, or cement-faced houses as white as those along
the coast of Morocco are said to be. These white
houses in their sand gardens are peculiarly effective;
their white fronts are never relieved by porch or cornice or portico or column, and the level white surface
is only relieved by those window boxes so common in
England, filled with yellow or pink or crimson flowers
that fairly scream at you in the lustiness of their colour.

Whether brick or cement, these homes are built
wall to wall, all exactly the same height and of the same
plainness and solidity and decorousness and reserve,
and have the same non-communicative aspect. Here
and there, among these miles and miles of houses
whose similar faces are only varied by occasional loops
of wisteria vine across the white or red, is a square or

two of villas. These, of course, are built more variously, with larger gardens and high brick walls and iron gateways under ivy-grown brick archways. It was in one of these high brick walls, the red top set with broken, jagged green glass set in hard cement to exclude night intruders, that I found the door of Sir Edward Burne-Jones's studio, called here the Garden Studio. The studio is built against the garden wall like a porter's lodge, with a street door, and another door into the garden, beyond which stands the house in which the painter lived. Lady Burne-Jones lets the house now, having changed her place of residence to Prince's Gate, Hyde Park, but she keeps the studio unchanged as her husband requested. We were admitted first into the vestibule, a little square place with a brick floor and whitewashed brick walls, where James, valet to Sir Edward's person and to his art, kept guard and still keeps guard, sitting the day long with his pipe and a copy of *Sporting Life*, watcher and warden still. The studio itself is a bare tank of a place, bare as a room could well be save for the beauty with which its walls are clad; long and narrow, so narrow that three standing abreast can reach from wall to wall, entirely windowless, with only the cold north light that streams in searchingly through the glass roof. There are perhaps a score of pictures in oil, finished and unfinished, and some hundreds of studies in crayon and black-and-white and sepia. To catalogue the names of pictures without accompanying reproductions is wearisome and profitless, and I will not attempt it. Among the finished pictures are the Venus Concordia and the companion Venus Discordia, a series of panels depicting the adventures of Perseus, and a Blind Love. To anyone who has ever come under the subtle and melancholy spell of Burne-Jones's work it is only necessary to say that all these things, from the slightest study of an arm to the finished pictures, are most really and wholly and convincingly his, and could be the conception or execution of no other man. Certainly there can be no question nowadays as to who was master of all English painters. It seems well established that he was the only painter the island has produced whose colour-sense can not be challenged, and, excepting Rossetti, he alone is unstained by that muck of sentimentality which has choked all truth and courage and vividness out of English art. There is something that speaks from every canvas or study on the studio wall, from the long-limbed languid women, the wide, far-seeing eyes, the astonishingly bold, yet always delicate and tender experiments in composition and colour scheme, which speak from no other canvas stretched in English land. For this grace of curve and pregnant beauty of line, this harmony between figure and setting, this depth of atmosphere and truth of tone and subtle poetry of colour, you can find no equal here.

It was James, the valet to the arts, who showed us the dozens of studies from which many of the well-known pictures grew. James is wide and red of countenance, with diminutive mutton chops and a keen grey eye, a very typical English gentleman's gentleman, who lived from his boyhood in Sir Edward's service.

"There," remarked James, "are the drawings Sir Edward made for Mr. Morris to illustrate the book of Chaucer. This set are for the Legend of Good Women, and there is Chaucer hisself lyin' asleep a-dreamin' of them. Here is a number of studies he made for the mermaid—everybody knows that paintin'. He had great trouble with the pose, and done them over a good bit, and here's the study for the head of the dead man she was draggin' under the sea. Models? Oh, no, he didn't often use the same one twice. He weren't particular, Sir Edward. Any model would do for him, and his studies was never like the models a bit when he'd done 'em. He knowed what he wanted his women to look like, he just used models for the pose merely, and the drapery. He never had no models for the face at all, just for crooks of the neck and shoulders and that. He knowed what he wanted. You won't find models lookin' like any of his heads, I fancy."

These are the words of James, faithfully set down, and I put them down because I wish to remember them, for it has not often been my good fortune to pass a summer afternoon with such a valet of such a hero. In reading a transcription of James's dissertation, however, it is necessary to entirely eliminate the letter "h" wherever it occurs, in order to get a correct idea of his speech. James's personal attitude I found interesting and perplexing; one could no more accuse him of having any sort of comprehension of painting than one could accuse him of any artistic temperament. Yet he is no fake of the sort who besets you at Stratford and chants, "Here died the immortal bard in 1616." James has no sepulchral tone, and no speeches fast committed. It is not his business to talk, and he is not a guide. Only friendly overtures and silver and a claim of mutual acquaintance drew him from his sombre silence. Once started, his enthusiasm carried him on. The source of his enthusiasm baffled me. He knew the name of the most meagre study, into what picture it had gone at last, how many times it had been done, and something of the technical difficulties it presented. He spoke of the vanquishing of these difficulties with a pride peculiar to the makers of things. He had somewhat to say of Watts and all the many and much-gifted Rossettis, and of the Morrises and Ford Madox Brown, whose daughter married D. G. Rossetti's brother. I would give James many bright sovereigns for his head full of recollections.

The picture Burne-Jones was working on when he died hangs in the studio. It is called "The Passing of Venus," and the realization of it seems to have caused him not a few low moments, for there are many impatient studies for it in chalk and crayon, and three canvases which were nearly finished and then thrown aside as inadequate. "It was one of them as went bad from the beginning, as some will, you know," said James. "But them was often Sir Edward's best. He was workin' on it of nights when he died, only then it stood over there where the big picture always stood." By the big picture James seemed to mean the picture on which the strain of labour fell. Whatever it happened to be, it was for James and Sir Edward "the big picture."

James planted his sturdy broad finger on one after another of the things of inspiration, and told us when and where and how, and neither his air of certainty nor his English offended. There was about him the undisputable conviction of an authority. He knew in what collection all Sir Edward's pictures are held, how they

were born, and where, and of the pain of their bearing. Yet he knew so little about art that he declared Sir
Edward's son "a foin portrait pynter." Nevertheless, I
would wager that James knows more about Burne-
Jones himself than any other person living knows, and
more about the road he trod, and what beset his soul
on the way. I suspect, too, that, were all the Burne-
Jones pictures in the world in danger of immediate
and utter destruction, James would risk his neck a
deal quicker than the painter's most soulful and pen-
etrating and comprehensive lovers. There is a warmer
note in James's admiration than in that of any enthusi-
ast I have ever talked with. The pictures are, in a fashion, his life works, and certainly his life interest. I can
only conjecture that, though his doors are shut and
heaven gave him no windows, yet James has been valet
to the arts so long, washed palettes and ground colours and stretched canvas, as well as the painter's trousers, that some of the radiance in which the painter
lived has got somehow in through the roof of James,
doorless and windowless as he is. As he talked, James
fell, after a time, into the lingo of the studio, into the
artist's way of measuring what part of the day was good
for anything, into the painter's peculiar anatomical
terms, and all this with never an "h" in his whole flow
of speech. Certainly James knows what he knows, and

has food for reflection when he wearies of *Sporting Life*. As he remarked with a smile and a shrug, "Livin' with artists all my life, I couldn't get on elsewhere, it's likely." Even though he never laid eyes on the high lady who in priceless moments was wont to come there, James may have felt something in the air and light and golden calm, and the silence of swift work, that told him she was there; and now that she keeps tryst no more, he sits with his paper and briar pipe and mounts guard before the little cell where once she came and went, while he fended off the pagan world from the holy moments that were hers.

I have spent some time in Watts's studio and in Rossetti's and in that house beautiful of Egyptian wood-work and Moorish tiles and priceless stone-work and glass-work from the Orient where Sir Frederick Leighton painted his pictures; but after these show studios Sir Edward's gloomy tank seems only the more richly clad with loveliness. Neither the high, clear tinkle of the fountain which sings incessantly in the stone-faced, shadowy Arabian hall at Leighton House, nor the balconies that hang over the little province of high-walled orchard, can altogether make one forget the pathetic ignominy of Leighton's canvases, where flesh of man, woman, and beast are of one texture with drapery, earth, and sky, and where all are lost in muddy colour and the rigidity and flatness of death. Rossetti's studio is now let to other hands and his sketches are scattered, though I have succeeded in finding one large collection. In Watts's studio only the portraits are worth serious study, and it is probable that he will hold his place among painters only through them. It was only in his portraits that he was wholly and only a painter, that he entirely escaped that passion for seeing and making sermons in paint which has been the damnation of English artists. The great majority of his pictures are interesting only because of their literary associations or the story they tell, and photographic reproductions of them are more satisfying than the originals. Even in a nightmare, the humblest Italian painter of any of the early schools could not have dreamed of such transgressions in colour as some of them present.

[7]

The Merry Wives of Windsor

To those unfamiliar with the amount of trenchant and uncompromising dramatic criticism that Willa Cather had already written for the columns of the Lincoln newspaper during her years at the university, this article given wholly to the review of a single play may seem exceptional. To Willa Cather herself it must merely have been a repetition, in Europe, of an already long familiar task.

Whatever crudities there may have been to life in Nebraska, there she had early known what the theater was like. The best actors of their day—Sarah Bernhardt, Modjeska, Julia Marlowe, Richard Mansfield, and Mrs. Patrick Campbell—all had played in Lincoln. There she had reviewed seasoned plays, and appraised many varieties of interpretation. So the qualities of a production by Mr. Beerbohm Tree, or of the acting of Ellen Terry with Mrs. Kendal, here in London, presented no unfamiliar challenge.

She acquits herself of it extremely well. She catches with delight what amounts to a great practical joke in those scenes juxtaposing the two "merry wives," given their well-known mutual hostility. We are informed of the rift; and of its apparent healing—at least on the stage—during this coronation year.

Willa Cather also describes the mounting of the play, to good effect. Now, though—we may observe— she can toss in a reference to the old houses of Chester or Ludlow, to make a point, with amusing ease. She mentions the spontaneity, the rough-and-tumble, of the stage action, and the obvious pleasure it gave the audience; and now richer by further experience in Paris, she contrasts with it the scrupulous unities of French construction.

With her old intransigeance, she berates Mr. Tree unhesitatingly for his expurgation of the text, which in her opinion diminishes not only his own stature as Falstaff, but even the proper effect of Shakespeare's play. The many cuts seem to her sheer prudery. "If the English have a national poet who cannot be read in public, then they are the only nation so unfortunate." Here is no timid girl from the provinces! Whatever diffidence Willa Cather may have felt in entering unfamiliar areas of English life, when she saw something that she judged inferior behind the footlights, there was no false modesty.

What in the end fixes her attention is, naturally enough, the acting of the merry wives themselves. With these rivals no overtone seems to escape her. Here on English soil, she senses a special Elizabethan quality to Ellen Terry's acting as Mistress Page, divining in its "romping spirit" and its "wildfire wit" an old and cheerful origin. Her whole analysis is subtle and cogent. No wonder we hear that when traveling companies went to Lincoln, in the old days, they came to dread the judgments of this forthright young critic.

In her first novel, Alexander's Bridge, written under Jamesian influence and dating from 1912, Willa Cather does indeed assign one of the chief roles to an English actress. This, still a decade away, is also her only long story with a predominantly metropolitan setting. Except incidentally, after this single delayed experiment, the dramatic stage finds little place in her stories.

She does, though, revert to it effectively on one

*other occasion, a piece of pure comedy in My Ántonia,
of 1918. There we have a masterly description of Ca-
mille, performed in Lincoln by an old-fashioned, medi-
ocre traveling company—yet seen through the eyes,
and with the unbounded extravagance and enthusiasm,
of youth. It gives us her sense of the theater, in all its
charm and absurdity, re-created after many years with
wonderful lightness of touch.*

Paris, August 8, 1902

PROBABLY no play has been produced in London
for some years which has proved so solid a financial
success as Mr. Beerbohm Tree's revival of *The Merry
Wives of Windsor*. The production was planned as a
feature of the coronation festivities, and though nearly
all such ventures miscarried, Mr. Tree's was and is a
marked exception. In the first place, people take pretty
much whatever comes to His Majesty's Theatre. In the
second, this production was interesting as a means that
at last brought about a truce between the two most
popular women on the English stage—Mrs. Kendal
and Ellen Terry. The breach between the two actresses
was of some twenty years' standing, and seemed likely

to endure until the end of their working days, for Mrs. Kendal is relentlessness itself, and Miss Terry is not overly prone to sue for pardon. But the coronation being an occasion of no little importance, and the King's interest in Mr. Tree's venture being known, the two ladies were got together and the terms of the peace arranged, Miss Terry being cast for the better of the two principal female parts.

The mechanical appurtenances of the production were superb. The costuming and the scenic embellishments were quite as artistic as any other features of the performance. The scenes laid in the village of Windsor gained considerable verity by reason of the careful reproduction of just such streets and buildings as one finds in Chester and Ludlow today, left over from Elizabethan days. One device which added greatly to the finish of the stage picture was the covering of the floor of the stage with a carefully wrought imitation of the cobble-stone streets of old Windsor.

As an acting play, it is not easy to pass a verdict on *The Merry Wives of Windsor*, or even to venture an opinion. It is a farce pure and simple, and a good deal of its humour is of the sort that children delight to watch in the circus ring. There is so much beating of bodies and staggering of the drunken, that one wonders whether Voltaire were not bearing this particular comedy in mind when he describes Shakespeare as a "drunken savage with glimpses of genius." Certainly, a comedy which presents three plots, no two of which have the remotest essential connection, could only seem a work of madness to any critic with a Latin feeling for form. What business Sir Hugh Evans and Dr. Caius have in the play at all is quite beyond the guessing of the ordinary playgoer. The only reasonable attitude of the spectator is to consider the play as one must consider certain English novels, without any reference to its form at all. The comedy seems to have been written merely as a farcical presentation of English village life, and the types were, as likely as not, taken from Stratford itself. This is not denying that the piece had its *raison d'être* in Sir John Falstaff, for the versatile knight might have graced almost any plot or been at home in any setting. Originally the comedy must have appealed to the British stomach by reason of its noise and cudgelling and broad jests, and largely because of the local colour and the title, which caught the ear of the London public as *The Merry Wives of New Yorkers* might that of New York today. Today people go to see it because it is lavishly staged in Mr. Tree's theatre, because such a revival is not likely to occur again for many years, because Falstaff has everywhere penetrated the public comprehension, and because London loves to vigorously applaud whenever Mrs. Kendal and Miss Terry embrace each other. Certainly, from *The Merry Wives of Windsor* as it is given now in London, no one could ever guess the author of *Twelfth Night* or *As You Like It*.

About Mr. Tree's expurgation of the comedy, there may be several opinions. Certainly the lines of Sir John himself are pruned away until there is little left of the character, and his aims and motives are alike unexplained. Mr. Tree argues that the knight's lines would necessarily offend a modern audience, so he presents a Falstaff whose resemblance to Shakespeare's goes little further than the paunch. Mr. Tree's argument recalls the story of the classic Mrs. Siddons's Rosalind. She wished to play the character, and she did not wish to incur the exposure of a page's costume, so she appeared in a sort of Highland kilt, which was quite too much even for the gravity of a London audience. Neither Mrs. Siddons nor Mr. Tree were compelled to revive Shakespearean comedies if they did not wish to, but it would seem as though, if they did present them, they ought to do it honestly. If the English have a national poet who cannot be read in public, then they are the only nation so unfortunate. When you hear a play of Molière's given at the Français, or sit through five interminable acts of *Ruy Blas* in which every line is given its full value, you begin to realize what respect for tradition means.

Mr. Tree's presentation of the fat knight can scarcely be termed anything but unfortunate. He plays the character with an earnestness which quite robs it of its flavour. His Falstaff takes himself with the utmost seriousness and is quite without the one saving grace of a keen sense of humour, which his creator certainly meant he should have. He comments upon the graces of his person with the utmost seriousness, which, even though it is most characteristically English, is tedious and absurd. When this Falstaff puts on the stag horns for his rendezvous in Windsor Forest, he does it as seriously as though he were donning a new doublet. Poor Sir John had faults enough, surely, and it is quite superfluous that Mr. Tree should add to the catalogue the crowning sin of grave stupidity. The farce ends in a masque, a fairy pantomime. After the husbands have made mirth at Sir John's expense in the forest, and the children have pinched and tweaked him, the dance begins. In their revel the merry wives acquit themselves right well, and poor Sir John renders tribute to English sentiment by admirably dancing with the children. The curtain falls on a jovial can-can between the fat knight and a little girl of six or seven, a touching picture of amiable and domestic old age, a scene of the Victor-Hugo-among-his-grandchildren order, which the French people are so partial to.

If the production is at all justified, it is the two merry wives who do it. The amount of sport which Mrs. Kendal as Mrs. Ford and Miss Terry as Mrs. Page get out of the wild and incongruous situation of the play well nigh makes one forget their absurdity. Both the ladies wear headdresses with heavy drapery about the throat and chin, which effectually conceals any ravages of relentless time and renders them delightfully youthful. Mrs. Kendal, indeed, never quite loses that dignity wherein she keeps her state, and it is fitting that Mrs. Ford should be the more reserved of these two honest, but merry, wives. But the spirit, the dash and gleam of the whole performance emanate from Ellen Terry. Neither a dull daughter nor a stolid Falstaff can daunt her. She plays as though she were seventeen yesterday; with an elasticity, a lightness, and a relish that might well have captivated even so dull a Falstaff. It is not her grace, her spirited reading, or her bounding step only that charm. She seemed the only player wholly in atmosphere, the only one who was imbued with the spirit of things Elizabethan. Now I believe I understand better that wildfire wit which has always baffled me. There is a bit of old England left in Ellen Terry. This play delights her as it delighted the spectators in the pit of the old playhouses. There is some of the strong old wine left in her, light of touch as she is, and under all her sweeping lines of grace there is something of the naïve, romping spirit which Shakespeare meant as the keynote of Mrs. Page and Mrs. Ford, those two very merry wives of Windsor. In her comedy there is just the faintest aroma of all that jumble of fisticuffing and jocular horseplay which for several centuries constituted English comedy. This is the warm, live heart of her harmonious and graceful art, and gives it the convincing and carrying power.

[8]

Dieppe and Rouen

In the following article we shall participate in Willa Cather's introduction to France, hours that for many Americans are often second in importance only to touching English soil, if that. Sensitively she describes the transition, the last of the lights of England, and finally, in the murky darkness, a first flare from the Norman coast. "Certainly so small a body of water as the English Channel never separated two worlds so different." She also in her turn must make this old discovery. At dawn, symbolically, we debark with her in another, rosy world.

She travels with humble people, and everywhere observes them closely; just as later, for instance, she will notice an immigrant family like the Shimerdas, at the beginning of My Ántonia, arrive in the West. Through some mysterious law, these simple figures always catch and retain her attention. This is true even as the two young women—with only a few hours of sleep behind them, for these are the travels of youth and energy— drive through the early-morning streets to their hotel in Dieppe. Even through her fatigue she notices an old woman ragpicker, and ponders on the activity and destinies of the whole tribe.

Then comes golden slumber; after which, at breakfast, here in good bright air again, she makes her first taste of Continental hotel life. The glass-enclosed dining-room, the yellow sands and blue sea beyond, are sketched as for a scene by the—as yet unknown— Marcel Proust. Here, "freshly created," her heart rides high as a boy's kite that she sees being flown from the hotel terrace.

She descends, quite obviously, to acquit herself of a few historical facts, for her readers. Yet after only a few sentences her other self breaks through once more, to enjoy her first French castle, picturing William the Conqueror, hearing the harness clank upon the knights riding with him along the road to near-by Arcques. To see such a setting was for her to re-people it, to reconstruct the past again. This will later become one of her powers.

That same afternoon, through the blond, tree-lined wheatfields of France, then even as now "sown thick with poppies," the two companions ride further to Rouen. Here, significantly, it is Gustave Flaubert and Guy de Maupassant, major figures in her literary pantheon, who are given first mention. It is wholly natural, one feels, for Willa Cather to apprehend a city chiefly in terms of its men of letters. She even would see it through their eyes; these were the serious values.

In Rouen, though, one other major impression, of architectural beauty, was to come within these next few hours; and then remain for years. She finds words of moving beauty to describe for us her first glimpse of the cathedral, its arches and its vaulting, the "burning blue and crimson" of its two great rose windows. This picture was to remain unaltered, clearly retained, over a very long period.

Twenty years later, in 1922, when she wishes to express the high meaning of France to Claude, the sensitive, diffident young boy from Nebraska who is to become the hero of One of Ours, she describes the sweet and awesome feelings that come over him, also here in Rouen, as silently he first walks down the aisles of an old Gothic church.

This is her great tribute to the art of medieval architecture, to what is finest in the Old World, and has endured; to all that elsewhere (in "The Sculptor's Funeral") she will describe as "chastened and old, and noble with traditions." Trait for trait, her description in One of Ours may be compared with the present passage. We could ask for no better example of her sensitiveness, her scale of values.

[Undated]

WE crossed from Newhaven to Dieppe on a night when the Channel ran smoothly as glass and the stars stood clear in the midnight sky. Soon after the long lines of the coast-wise lights of England had quite died away, the sky clouded, and except where a pale star here and there struggled through, there was nothing to break the common blackness of the sea and sky. If one stared hard enough and long enough it was possible to divine the horizon line rather than see it. The boat was crowded, and the wind blew cold, and the decks were peopled with miserable shivering Latins who had not secured staterooms and crouched under rubber blankets. When we quitted the decks at about one o'clock in the morning, they were scenes of chill and heaviness and discomfort. About three o'clock, however, I heard a rush of feet aft, and, tumbling into my ulster and mufflers, hurried out to see what had occasioned the excitement. Above the roar of the wind and thrash of the water I heard a babble of voices, in which I could only distinguish the word "France" uttered over and over again with a fire and fervour that was in itself a panegyric. Far to the south there shone a little star of light out of the blackness, that burned from orange to yellow and then back to orange again; the first light of the coast of France. All the prone, dispirited figures we left two hours before were erect and animated, rhetorical and jubilant. They were French people from all over the world: women who had been teaching French in the United States; girls who had been governesses in England; journeymen tailors and workers at various handicrafts. They clutched and greeted each other indiscriminately, for it was the hour when all distinctions were obliterated and when the bond of brotherhood drew sweet and hard. Above all the ardent murmurings and the exclamations of felicity, there continually rose the voice of a little boy who had been born on a foreign soil and who had never been home. He sat on his father's shoulder, with his arms locked tight about his neck, and kept crying with small convulsions of excitement, "Is it France? Is it France?" No wonder a Parisian speaks so pityingly

when he says of certain ones of the Bourbon family,
"He died in exile."

By the time the first excitement was over a dozen
lights outlined the coast, and then the dawn began to
come up. The black water broke in long-lashed, regular waves toward the shore. The sky was black behind
us and grey before, a yellow crescent of the old moon
hung just over the red lighthouse top. The high chalk
cliffs of Normandy were a pale purple in the dim light.
Little fishing boats passed us continuously, their ragged sails patched with red and blue. When we touched
the dock the sky, the gravel beach, the white town,
were all wrapped in a pale pink mist, and the narrow
streets were canals of purple shadows. Certainly so
small a body of water as the English Channel never
separated two worlds so different. In the railway station here every poster was a thing of grace and beauty.
The very porters spoke in smooth, clear voices that
phrased the beautiful tongue they spoke almost as music is phrased. The cries of the street boys were musical.

As we drove to our hotel we passed only workmen
and market folks and one old ragpicker in wooden
shoes and skirts almost up to her knees, who looked
hungrily at us out from under her white cap as she
fished with her stick in the gutter. Surely there is no
other country where there are so many aged women, or

where they retain their activity so long. When we arrived at our hotel we were too sleepy to notice anything except that the entire front of the building was glass, that the beach before it was very yellow and the sea very blue. When we awoke and revisited the world about eight o'clock, everyone else seemed to feel as happy and as freshly created as ourselves. In the glass dining-room where we breakfasted there were many flowers and a few smiling people. The childen were running up and down the beach with their nurses. The sanded yards were splashed here and there with beds of red geraniums. The last of the fishing boats were dipping below the horizon. The purple chalk cliffs were dazzling white now, and our eyes, accustomed for some weeks to the blackness of London, ached with the glare of the sun on the white stone and yellow sand. A little boy on the stone terrace was flying a red and green kite, quite the most magnificent kite I have ever seen, and it went up famously, up and up until his string ran short, and of a truth one's heart went just as high.

Dieppe today subsists chiefly through marine industries. From time immemorial the men of the town have been famous seamen, and have divided their energies between fishing and hating the English. Their boats go to Norway and Sweden for lumber, and to

Newfoundland and Iceland for fish. The shores are
full of drying nets and fishing boats a-mending. Among
the great navigators born and bred there were Jean
Cousin and Jean Ribault, who was massacred by the
Spaniards in Florida. The town, because of its hardy
seamen and venturesome spirit, was peculiarly fa-
voured by most of the French kings, particularly by
Francis I. Louis XIV was its worst enemy and nearly
ruined the place through taxation because so many of
the Huguenots escaped through their port. The *château* at Dieppe is not so interesting as that at Arques, a
few miles distant. The Château d'Arques is the ruins
of a Norman structure of gigantic proportions which
stands upon the top of a chalk hill beside the river
Arques. In this chalk cliff there are cut tunnels which
give egress to various points along the coast and were
invaluable in the long sieges the castle often sustained.
Some of these underground passages are twenty-five
miles long. Only a little boy, however, or a Robert
Louis Stevenson, could understand or set forth the ro-
mantic possibilities of these winding tunnels or the
thrice-walled and moated structure from which they
lead. One so happily gifted might lie of a sunny morning on the smooth decline of the grassy moat and hear
the harness clank upon the knights riding, with William the Norman at their head, down the long white

road that winds up to the castle on the hill. They keep William's portrait at the castle still, and the restless, scornful, unhappy face of him seems an impossible product for that kindly, cheerful Norman country.

That afternoon we rode away through miles of brook-fed valleys and yellow wheat fields sown thick with poppies, and tall Lombard poplars and pale willows and grey elms, such as Corot and Puvis de Chavannes so often painted. Late in the day we arrived at Rouen, the well-fed, self-satisfied *bourgeois* town built upon the hills beside the Seine, the town where Gustave Flaubert was born and worked, and which he so sharply satirized and bitterly cursed in his letters to his friends in Paris. In France it seems that a town will forgive the man who curses it if only he is great enough. One of the first things that greet your eye in Rouen is the beautiful monument erected to Flaubert in the very wall of the Museum, which is Rouen's holy of holies. Just across the walk from him, in front of a dense cluster of sycamore trees, is his friend and pupil Guy de Maupassant. The Maupassant statue at Rouen is, I think, quite as impressive as that in Paris—perhaps more so—and it is even more happily placed. Besides, there is something very fitting in the idea of commemorating together the master and the pupil who surpassed him.

It happened to be the afternoon when the children had been for their examination in catechism, and as we crossed tree-lined squares we met troops of them, each wearing a wreath and each bearing a prize, for the happy feature of these catechism contests seems to be that everyone gets a share of the honour. I am unable to believe statistics as to the stationary population of France. I never saw so many children anywhere as I have seen in Paris and the northern towns; no, nor such pretty children nor such happy ones.

The most beautiful thing about Rouen is the stillness and whiteness and vastness of its cathedral. The exterior is by no means so fine as that of the beautiful church of St. Ouen, which stands near it, but the interior is vested with a peace that passes understanding. The columns and arches are beautifully fluted and of the most delicate and slender Gothic, vault after vault rising high and effortless as flame. The uniform whiteness of the walls and arches and high, slender columns is varied by the burning blue and crimson of two rose windows almost as beautiful as those of Nôtre Dame. The place is so vast that even the vesper service could be heard only near the altar, and so dusky that the lighted tapers cast dancing reflections on the white stone. All the light streams from windows so high that one seems to look up at them from the bottom of a well. Behind the choir is a reclining figure of Richard Cœur-de-Lion, and under it is the urn in which his heart was placed. On every side of him is dim, rich light and a very forest of white, slender stone columns, with silence absolute and infinitely sweet. There could scarcely be a better place for so hot a heart to rest.

[9]

The Cemeteries of Paris

We may wonder a little why two young women exploring France should wish to spend precious summer days in Paris amid the gravel and carved stones of Montmartre and Père-Lachaise. In 1902, however, the general sightseer was perhaps more earnest about such matters than he seems to be today; and Willa Cather herself was also drawn by her real worship of great writers, the honored dead, whose work for so long had made the richness and meaning of her life.

Although, she is smilingly aware, "a really appreciative attitude toward Paris cemeteries is well-nigh impossible to anyone but a Frenchman," she promptly sets about to describe their incongruities for her Nebraska readers, pinning down the oddities, although in writing obviously hasty. In the cemetery of Mont-martre, the great—familiar to her by their lives as well as their works—are everywhere: the brothers Goncourt, Alexandre Dumas the younger, even Alphonsine Ples-sis, the Lady of the Camellias. Heine seems specially to attract her; she had been familiar with his verse, we know, from early years. The earnest girl from the Divide has a wide range. She came well prepared.

Turning to Père-Lachaise, she is at once fascinated by a great group of sculpture, which—although she does not here name it—is the well-known Monument aux Morts by Paul-Albert Bartholomé. Dating from 1895, this had been conceived in deep sorrow—the loss of the sculptor's adored young wife; and these facts she presumably found in her guidebook.

Here we can trace her full-scale contemplation, in Europe, of a subject that was never afterward to leave her: the mystery and meaning of life and its end. Her brooding on the sad figures going so inevitably toward the tomb, and their final transmutation once they have passed beyond its threshold, is intense. Sculpture here symbolizes her greatest theme, in stories and novels yet unborn.

Indeed, death—which, in the verses she admired, came so regularly for the Housman lads and lasses—will in the future claim as its own many if not most of the figures in her own pages. Even at the beginning, in 1905, there is the sculptor whose funeral will make the title to his story in The Troll Garden. In the same book, " 'A Death in the Desert' " will deal with a similar tragedy, this time of a singer; while "Paul's Case," which concludes it, inevitably ends in suicide.

The hero of Alexander's Bridge, of 1912, is fated to meet his death by a long unrecognized flaw in his own nature. There is a double death, under tragic circumstances, of Emil with Marie Shabata in O Pioneers! of the following year. In The Song of the Lark, 1915, Ray Kennedy, the railwayman, must perish before Thea can have her precious chance to study, with a small legacy that only death releases. Anton Shimerda, also, unable to endure the burden of wresting a living from a too alien world, takes his own life in My Ántonia, of 1918.

Contemplation of death—as time goes on—comes to occupy even the central place in Willa Cather's thinking. Claude, in One of Ours, of 1922, seems even from the first fated to die. The title of The Professor's House, 1925, denotes finally his own only real home, which is his grave. My Mortal Enemy, of the following year, is a grim—indeed fierce—tale about the difficulties even of dying. The dread word moves into the title of her next novel, Death Comes for the Archbishop, of 1927.

It would become wearisome to pursue such a list in too great detail; yet it includes many of her chief later characters. There is Frontenac, for instance, in Shadows on the Rock, of 1931; then both "Neighbour Rosicky" and "Old Mrs. Harris"—here she reaches sublimity—must meet death, in the stories that bear their names, published in 1932. A further heroine, Lucy Gayheart, in the novel of 1935, is early marked for tragedy; and the man she loves is drowned. There are even others—"The Old Beauty," and also the young schoolteacher in "The Best Years," in two stories published posthumously, in 1948.

The hardness of life, and its inevitable end, thus quite dominate Willa Cather's mature writing; and here, on her first journey to Paris, we can see her suddenly transfixed, pondering the meaning of the great mystery as it was revealed through art in an unexpected and appealing work of contemporary French sculpture.

This natural sensitiveness to plastic beauty she was never to lose. After her first experiments it may not take the form of direct reference to sculpture itself. As we have seen, music will become, in her novels, the preferred art. Yet whether it be a Mexican house, fashioned on its native earth in adobe, or a mesa standing brilliant and aloof under Southwestern sunlight; the winding lanes of a gray French town perched in the snow upon Canadian rock; or even details—a primitive Indian pot, some wild bush, a flower: whatever she undertakes to describe seems first to have been grasped, by her mind, "in the round." Willa Cather was incapable of mere delineation.

To end her article, and as if for contrast, she turns to the grave of another familiar, Alfred de Musset, quite enjoying the literary origin of the spindly and rather absurd willow, planted by his request, that she finds growing above it. Finally, we have Félix Faure, Chopin, and Balzac; she will appraise and pass them all in review!

Turning back to the streets of Paris, on her departure we find her still dreaming of "victory—either of arms or intellect." She is busy appraising life, what it gives of fame and glory; but, above all, for all of earth's children, even the most talented, what it can withhold. She has begun her long meditation upon its brevity, and its end.

Paris, August 21, 1902

THE cemetery of Montmartre has one of the most beautiful situations in Paris. The hill of Montmartre towers above the rest of the city like one of those cloud-topped volcanoes in children's geography books. On the very summit of the hill rises the church of Sacré-Cœur, largest of all modern churches, and a hill in itself. The church is all of white stone, with round Byzantine towers and dome. If one approaches Paris from the north the white gleam of Sacré-Cœur is the first thing that strikes the eye, and on a sunny day the rest of the city, below, lies bathed in a violet light, with here and there white towers. From the terrace at St. Germain, Montmartre, with the purple city below, looks like the city of St. John's vision, or the Heavenly City that Bunyan saw across the river. Montmartre is one of the most picturesque quarters of Paris, and of late years has been much affected by painters and poets and political theorists, who have colonized there from the Latin Quarter. The Moulin Rouge is there, and the narrow streets leading down from Sacré-Cœur were favourite haunts of Baudelaire and Paul Verlaine. The roadways and narrow streets are cobble-paved, built up on either side with ancient stucco houses, with here and there a walled garden. These garden walls are all overgrown with wisteria, and tall sunflowers nod over them. The effect of these high old houses with straight wall-like fronts, rising on either side of the narrow streets into the high, pale blue Paris sky, is in itself very singular. The effect is heightened by the vines that trail over the white fronts of the houses, and the brilliant flowers that grow wherever there is a spot of earth to bear them. A little below these picturesque streets lies one of the two great burial grounds of Paris. A really appreciative attitude toward Paris cemeteries is well-nigh impossible to anyone but a Frenchman. There is not a blade of grass anywhere in them, the entire enclosures being covered with gravel, which is occasionally raked to keep it loose. I heard an American girl remark that "it seemed exactly like burying people in a tennis court." The trees are very beautiful and carefully kept, but there is no low, green tent for the Paris dead. Their relatives heap over them great masses of stone, most of which are monstrosities of taste. These heavy, sombre piles are decorated with the most objectionable artificial flowers and dozens of wreaths, anchors, cornucopias, etc., made of brilliantly coloured glass beads strung on wire. Some of the tombs are decorated with immense wreaths of painted china roses, weighing a dozen pounds or so.

In their death as in their life the Latins are more socially disposed than we, and the graves in their cemeteries almost always touch each other, they are so closely crowded together. Occasionally flowers or shrubs are planted about the tombs, but for the most part they are mere unsightly masses of stone, decorated with glass and tin wreaths, with narrow gravel walks running about them. The general effect strongly suggests a tennis court converted into a graveyard.

Marked exceptions to the generally execrable taste exhibited in Paris cemeteries are the tombs of its great men, which are usually very impressive. One of the first of these tombs that I found in Montmartre was that to the brothers Goncourt, a flat stone with bronze medallions. The tomb of Alexandre Dumas *fils* is by Saint-Marceaux, and is one of the most beautiful in the cemetery. The dramatist lies full length on the top of the flat stone, under a marble canopy. He is clad in his dressing gown, his feet bare, his head noble and calm. On the stone about him are carved camellia flowers in low relief. On the canopy above him is an inscription from one of his works: "I am keenly interested in my life, which pertains to time, but I am more interested in my death, which pertains to eternity." On the other side of the cemetery is the grave of Alphonsine Plessis, the original of *La Dame aux camélias*. She died in 1845, but there were a few flowers upon her grave a week ago, which speaks volumes for the inborn and unblushing sentimentality of Parisians. Far be it from them to miss such an opportunity! One of the tombs most often visited is that of Heinrich Heine and his wife, Mathilde. The tomb is surmounted by a bust of the poet, made from his later photograph, not the rotund, cynical face of the young Henry Heine, but a man grave and wan, with the clutch of pain upon him, whom the "Aristophanes of the universe" was already outdoing in irony. The head is a little bowed, as though the weight of life had bent the proud neck of the poet of scorn. On the day I saw the grave it was almost covered with bunches of blue forget-me-nots. Heine died in 1856, but the youth of the world, seemingly, remembers him still. The flowers were probably from some young German sojourning in Paris; certainly they were a tribute from youth, for the melody of Heine's verse never rings quite so true as in the years that lie the other side of twenty. Probably the youth of countless generations to come will exultantly discover him, feverishly read him, and passionately proclaim him. Scarcely a schoolboy will ever stand for the first time before the Venus de Milo in the Louvre without remembering that a death-struck Jew once sobbed his adieu to life there.

The cemetery of Père-Lachaise is the largest in Paris. The great monument to the dead there is one of the noblest works of modern sculpture. It is a great wall of white marble, set against a green hillside, representing a wall in the middle of which is a door. This door is literally the door to the tomb. On either side of this door are emaciated figures, life-sized or larger, who are being driven all unwillingly toward the dreaded portal. These figures are in every attitude of despair and opposition; one woman is bowed with her head upon the ground, one is kissing her hand in a despairing adieu to her friends in the world; another, a strong young man is trying to hold back. The male figures are equally unwilling; young men bowed with chagrin at their own physical weakness, old men who clutch the very stones with their toes in their pitiful effort to remain yet a little while in the happy world of living things. The realistic treatment of the sculptor has been now and then bitterly criticized, and people have found the horror of these struggling figures too poignant. It would seem, however, that they in reality only heighten the enviable repose of the central and emphatic figure of the work. There are two figures, a man and a woman, who have actually passed the portal, who are erect in the doorway, passing into the mystery that awaits them. No shrinking, no horror, no distortion or contraction there. They stand upright and calm: fearless, indifferent, and weary. Once inside the portal there is no fear, no longing for the backward path. Below this there is a crypt in which lie a nude

man and woman, their stiffened hands feebly inter-
locked, and across their bodies lies that of a chubby little child. It is to all Adam's seed, this monument, to
the human family and all its dead of the ages. Not to
artist or statesman or warrior, but to man, out of dust
fashioned, to woman, made to replenish the earth, and
to the children she has borne. The simplicity and vastness of the conception cannot be described in words,
and no pictorial reproduction gives one any adequate
idea of it.

The tomb of Alfred de Musset is one of the most
carefully kept in Père-Lachaise, and will be, so long as
the Panthéon stands and fickle-hearted youth awakens
in the Latin Quarter from dreams of glory. When the
boy from the provinces first comes up to Paris, after
quaking his way under the gold dome of the Invalides,
he makes his pilgrimage to the tomb of the poet who
sang all his ambitions, all his callow cynicism, all his
self-inflicted torments. There are almost always fresh
flowers lying before the bust of the poet, and below the
bust runs an inscription in verse to this effect:

> Friends of mine, when I shall die,
> Plant a willow over me.
> In its sad shade would I lie,

Its pallid leaf is dear to me.
Light its tender shade will weep
O'er the earth where I shall sleep.

This willow requested by the poet has become a subject of mirth even among Parisians, whose sense of the
ridiculous is almost entirely lacking. Ever since 1857
gardener after gardener has tried to make a willow tree
grow over the tearful singer's grave, but the soil of
Père-Lachaise is high and sandy, and the result of fifty
years of effort is a spindling yellow seedling, five feet
high, so nearly dead that its shade is as light as even so
sensitive a gentleman could have wished it. De Musset
certainly never got anything that he wanted in life,
and it seems a sort of fine-drawn irony that he should
not have the one poor willow he wanted for his grave.
On the other hand, no one ever quite so thoroughly
enjoyed the idea of missing all he wanted, and the con-
dition of this willow would certainly delight his artistic
sense as a most effective instance of the relentlessness
of a destiny of which he was never tired of complaining.

The monument to the late Félix Faure, by Saint-
Marceaux, is a striking example of the dignity that
modern realistic sculpture has attained. The president
lies at full length, in bronze, his head slightly turned.

He is in evening dress, with the broad ribbon of the Legion of Honour across his breast. The details of his costume are simply worked out, even the silk facing on his coat, yet it is absolutely free from any suspicion of triviality. The lower part of the body is draped in the flag of France. The tomb of Frédéric Chopin is also carefully kept. Over a medallion of the composer weeps a muse with her lyre. Balzac's monument is conspicuously ugly and deserted, but Balzac seems more a living fact than a dead man of letters. He lives in every street and quarter; one sees his people everywhere. The city of grey stone and stucco, interlaced by its clear green river and planted with sycamores and poplars, dominated by Nôtre Dame and the Invalides and the columns of victory, is no more real a thing than the great city of thought which Honoré de Balzac piled and heaped together and left, a ruin of chaotic magnificence, beside the Seine.

He told the story, not only of the Paris of yesterday, but of the Paris of today and tomorrow. Whatever changes take place in one's scale of estimates in Paris, the figure of that barbarian of letters looms larger and larger, until he seems second only to Napoleon himself. It was Balzac himself who used to wander in the Père-Lachaise in the days of his hard apprenticeship, reading the names on the tombs of the great. "Single names," he wrote his sister, "Racine, Molière, etc.; names that make one dream." Surely none among all the names there calls up visions more vast. None better earned the right to lie among the dead "whom," as a contemporary French writer puts it, "Paris loved so well; whom Paris forgets so soon."

The French people have a rather better way of commemorating their great men than building monuments to them—though there is a monument in every square and a dozen in every park—and that is naming their streets after them. This seems, some way, to keep the men still in the mouths of the living, to make their names still mean something in the big, stirring life of the common people. There is a rue Balzac and rue Racine and rue Molière, as well as a Place Wagram and a rue Arcola. Nearly every street in Paris bears the name of a victory—either of arms or intellect.

[10]

Barbizon

As with many of the others, there are passages in this article on Barbizon that show obvious haste. The series as a whole seems to have been dashed off—the impression grows—even penciled, as opportunity offered. Perhaps it was between projects, or returning from some new discovery, written on some humble table—while life, fresh life, was calling on every side. This was no time, nor was a Lincoln newspaper the place, for deliberate and carefully polished prose. What mattered, at present, was what was new!

The reader, though, able to look forward and see what is to come—even across a lifetime—is in a favored position. This first stay in France was for Willa Cather a time of impressions that went deep. Here at Barbizon, for instance, we are shown landscapes that will come to actuality again only in One of Ours, her war novel of 1922, twenty years later.

The wheatfields about the little village at the edge of the forest she seizes knowingly. They simply remind her of the "country about Campbell and Bladen." This is land that she can understand because it has an agricultural base, with a need for the continuous hard labor that she had known from girlhood.

Yet she also finds a France that is totally different, which twenty years later she will transpose into her soldier hero's first glimpses, in the little village where, also come from Nebraska, he will be billeted on his own first days there. One by one she dwells on details, what is significant for her at present—and later will also be for him. She takes delight in telling us of the courtyard at the inn, and the great horse chestnut there under which good food and wine are enjoyed, in the open, as seems possible only in France. In the novel of 1922 we have almost the whole description, even to the buildings along the single village street, once more. To be sure, the spreading tree in the later—quite unplaced—village will become a cherry; but its genesis, even to a threatening summer shower from which it offers shelter, is probably here, halfway across France.

As always, Willa Cather is quick to notice human

material, especially those who strive and are burdened
—here the laborers in the fields. And of these she picks
for special mention, once again, the old women.
"There is something worth thinking about," she finds,
in these lives; and this turns out to be, typically, the
combination of their valiant adequacy, at hard and sustained labor, with a passionate love for the abiding values of culture, in part here simply represented, very
cleverly, by good handwriting. This makes them true
cousins of the grandmothers she has known, even in
far-off Nebraska, on the Divide.

It is people like this, both men and women, who will
make a procession through her life. In almost every
novel it is they who carry the burden of the story. They
triumph over destiny, or are beaten in the struggle to
keep higher values amid surrounding difficulties.

All of us see only what by our own nature and personal experience we are destined to see; and Willa
Cather is no exception. Evening finds her still in the
late summer fields, thinking of Millet. To France as a
whole she has brought her feeling for the land, and
also much solid knowledge of French culture. How
just, then, is her intuitive penetration of these—also
"obscure"—destinies! So we find her as she returns to
her shelter at the inn, "through winding streets where
tired women sat on the wooden doorsteps, singing

tired children to sleep." Style fits words to sense, with precision; her writer's power is coming.

Masterfully she then shifts the mood, from pathos to rapid comedy. Her account of the Gallic animation at supper under the great tree arrives like a new musical theme, a sudden allegro con brio—enhanced with even a bit of a humorous galop—after a brooding adagio. This is one of the powerful unconscious effects, no doubt, that even at this time music has made upon her style. She has juxtaposed two quite different moods, and balanced them. Finally, her late walk in the moonlit forest, to end the day, draws her back to her original theme.

A few more random observations close the account; but the stage has been set for later work. We see this France, this life, becoming a part of her own. It will later give to Claude the meaning even of his existence. As she leaves her little village, we find her still watching the brave old peasant women across the sunset fields; and their homely chatter as they plod across the stubble, she tells us, "made the best kind of music in our ears."

Paris, September 10, 1902 *

As it is impossible to reach Barbizon by railway, we left the train at the town of Fontainebleau, which lies well in the forest of Fontainebleau. The palace of Fontainebleau is chiefly interesting through its souvenirs of Henry IV, Francis I, and Napoleon. There we saw Napoleon's bed, the table on which he signed his abdication, the grand portico from which he said adieu to the grand army, and his little throne, with the back round like a drum. We lunched at a place called the Cordon Bleu, which was thronged with bicyclers. In Fontainebleau is the only monument I have yet seen in a French park which seemed in bad taste. The monument is to Rosa Bonheur, and consists of an immense bronze bullock mounted on a pedestal. On the pedestal one finds, at length, a small bas-relief of the painter's virile face, but the first impression the monument gives is startling and somewhat shocking. From Fontainebleau we drove some five or six miles through the forest to Barbizon.

The village of Barbizon is a little place of one street, which street begins in Fontainebleau forest and ends

* This, most probably, is a misprint; perhaps for September 1.

in a wheat field. It was originally a wretched little set-
tlement of peasants, who came to till the few acres of
open land which happened to occur hereabout in the
great forest. The tireless admiration of Millet, Rousseau, and a few fellow artists made the place a rendezvous of artists from all over the world. Yet when you
drive through the one crooked street of the town, between the two rows of low, straw-roofed stucco houses,
and the garden wall covered with grapevine, it is hard
to believe that for thirty years painters, littérateurs, and
musicians have lived and worked there for months together. The first care of all these people has been to
leave intact the beauty that first drew them there.
They have built no new and shining villas, introduced
no tennis courts, or golf links, or electric lights. They
have even heroically denied themselves any sewage sys-
tem whatever, and the waste water from the kitchens
and water tubs flows odorously along through the
streets. The village at first sight looks like any other little forest town; the home of hard-working folk, desper-
ately poor, but never so greedy or so dead of soul that
they will not take time to train the peach tree against
the wall until it spreads like a hardy vine, and to mass
beautiful flowers of every hue in their little gardens. If
you look closely you will presently see the skylight of

little mud-walled studios here and there—Millet's and
Rousseau's the poorest and barest among them.

We had decided to stop at the Hôtel des Artistes,
which, though rather less interesting than Les Char-
mettes, is rather more reputable for women travelling
alone. We entered the hotel through a stone-paved
court, which led into the garden, completely enclosed
by the various wings of the rambling home. This garden, and it was no small one, was almost entirely
roofed by an enormous horse-chestnut tree, under
which several dozen small tables were placed. Our
rooms faced upon this garden, and we were sheltered
from the afternoon sun by the boughs of this mighty
tree. In the late afternoon we walked to the end of the
little street. The further we went from the hotel, the
more simple and primitive did the houses become; little huts of mud and stone, draped with vines and made
less gloomy by a clump of poppies or marigolds flam-
ing upon the roof. Two-wheeled carts, grindstones,
scythes, rakes, and various implements of husbandry
were strewn about the doors of the dwellings. The
wheat fields beyond the town were quite as level as
those of the Nebraska divides.

The long, even stretch of yellow stubble, broken

here and there by a pile of Lombard poplars, recalled
not a little the country about Campbell and Bladen,
and is certainly more familiar than anything I have
seen on this side the Atlantic. To complete the resemblance, there stood a reaper of a well-known American
make, very like the one on which I have acted as super-
cargo many a time. There was a comfortable little
place where a child might sit happily enough between
its father's feet, and perhaps if I had waited long
enough I might have seen a little French girl sitting in
that happy, sheltered place, the delights of which I
have known so well. The fields already cut were full of
stackers; men in their long blue blouses that hang
about their knees like shirts, and women bare-headed
and brown-faced and broad of shoulders. They all wore
wooden shoes, their skirts were high above the ankle,
and few of them wore stockings. After the rakers and
stackers came the gleaners—usually women who looked
old and battered, who were bent and slow and not
good for much else. Such brave old faces as most of
these field-working women have, such blithe songs
they hum, and such good-humoured remarks they
bawl at a girl who sees too much of one particular
reaper. There is something worth thinking about in
these brown, merry old women, who have brought up
fourteen children and can outstrip their own sons and

grandsons in the harvest field, lay down their rake and
write a traveller directions as to how he can reach the
next town in a hand as neat as a bookkeeper's. As the
sun dropped lower, the merriment ceased, the women
were tired and grew to look more and more as Millet
painted them, warped and bowed and heavy. The
horses strained in their harness, the ringdove began to
call mournfully from the pine wood in the west, and I
found there was a touch of latent homesickness in the
wide, empty, yellow fields and the reaper with the cozy
seat which some little brown-skinned Barbizon girl
would have tomorrow. Storm clouds were piling themselves up about the gorgeous sunset, and we tramped
silently back to Barbizon, through the winding street
where tired women sat on the wooden doorsteps, singing tired children to sleep.

Dinner was being served when we reached the Hôtel
des Artistes, which hostelry derives its very attractive
name from the fact that it has a studio to let, and that
the walls of the bar are decorated with oil sketches,
furnished mostly by painters who were unable to pay
their accounts. White cloths were laid on the little tables under the big horse-chestnut, and the six homely
daughters of the proprietor were running about calling,
"Red wine or white, monsieur?" Soon after we were

seated a few drops of rain fell, and although they did not penetrate the sheltering leaves of the great tree, such exclamations of woe and alarm arose from guests and servitors that you might have conjectured an earthquake was approaching, or that rain had never fallen in Barbizon before. The changing skies are one of the chief beauties of the forest, and in a few minutes the clouds had entirely disappeared. Then the gas lamp that hung from the boughs of the chestnut was lighted, and the dinner proceeded merrily.

Our fellow guests were an interesting lot of people. There were several French families who had come out to Barbizon to spend Sunday, and they were amused at everything and delighted with everything. There was a miserable, snaky little painter, with black hair and beard, whom we had often seen in the Latin Quarter. He wore his usual black felt hat and long black necktie, with sash-like ends that fell almost to his waist. He had his sweetheart with him, a rather pretty girl who wore powder and a preposterously small waist. We had noticed them in Paris, strolling arm in arm through the Luxembourg Gardens. Next day we saw him in the forest painting busily and leaving the sweetheart to her own devices. There were several other artists, older men and of a sturdier type, and an English bridal couple. The bride had visited the village before, we gathered, and had singled it out as the properest kind of a place for a honeymoon. The groom entertained her busily through dinner, breakfasted alone next morning, and was very much afraid that people might think that he was but recently married. The waitresses, who brought our order on the run from the first course, had reached a mad gallop by the time the coffee appeared. Everybody was particularly gay, and for no particular reason. Because the moon was soon to rise, forsooth, or because there were such fine green chestnut trees in the world, and such good salads in that happy part of the world called France. The painter looked at his wasp-waist lady as though she were a goddess, and the mamma of the Frémont family smiled at her daughters, who were uttering feeble witticisms to the sons of the Picard family, and wondered however she came to have such clever daughters. Père Picard and Père Frémont were telling each other stories of their conscript days in the army, and roaring, each at his own anecdotes. Oh, we were a motley, clever, self-appreciative lot of people at Barbizon that night, and it was a good world we lived in.

The conversation grew less animated, and we sat for a long time watching the glorious rising of the harvest moon before going for a walk through the moon-lit avenues of the forest. After sunset there is not a light in Barbizon, except here and there from a cottage window.

The next day we spent in the forest, walking all morning through the western section of it. Sometimes we kept to the white roads under the arching elms, and sometimes we went for miles over the blossoming heather, and again over glades of slippery pine needles or clambered over masses of tumbled rocks. It was at Barbizon and in the forest about, as all English-speaking people well remember, that Robert Louis Stevenson first met and became enamoured of the woman whom he afterward married in California. Certainly, if there is any spot in the world where a young man might be flung headlong into the most extravagant romance, it would be the forest of Fontainebleau. The old spell seems still to hold good, for we met occasionally a Columbine and her Pierrot. But much more often we encountered the one institution which you can never get away from in France—the family. Old men playing with their grandsons, young men walking with their mothers, sisters hand in hand, brothers arm in arm. They stopped to name every wild flower, they held hands and spanned the girth of all the big trees. What a fine tree to hide behind if a bear should come, said grandpa, and grandma and the young people laughed and called him a famous comedian, a regular Coquelin of a fellow. We were rather startled once at hearing a rollicking drinking song, by male and female voices, coming toward us through the wood, but it was only a *bourgeois* papa, his white waistcoat on; mamma stout and puffing as she plodded, her skirts held up under her elbow; and half a dozen sons and daughters, who were singing for joy of life and companionship.

That night we left Barbizon, unwillingly enough. When we drove away at about sunset, the harvesters were still working in the fields, and the chatter of the brave old peasant women who plodded across the stubble made the best kind of music in our ears.

[11]

Avignon

Reluctant as the two women seem to leave Paris behind, and wearying as becomes their long railway journey southward in a fusty and crowded third-class compartment, something quite extraordinary seems to
happen to Willa Cather as soon as for the first time
she enters the Midi. She notes at once the changes in
the countryside; the power of the swift-flowing Rhone
("none of your English streamlets"), the generous,
red-roofed farmsteads, the vine and the olive, all the
rich growth of the soil. Botany is as always an immediate, enduring interest. Here, though, beyond anything
she has read in Daudet, is wonderful discovery!

It is bliss to install herself in a hotel of character
such as she finds in Avignon—good enough to have

won praise, she remembers, even from Henry James. "People know how to live in this country"; her surmise runs deep. The dining-room, converted from a Gothic chapter house, and the first lavish meal of generous Provençal cooking only confirm her satisfaction. This unalloyed pleasure in succulent food will be developed over the years, in her writing, until in Death Comes for the Archbishop and Shadows on the Rock it becomes a symbol even for the nourishment of Latin culture.

In unhurried 1902, of course, such pleasures could be more tranquilly savored than in midsummer today. Our two travelers find themselves the only English-speaking tourists in the whole town! So one can fancy them wandering unimpeded about the quiet and orderly streets, exploring the fabric of the great palace of the popes, its architecture nobly bare, perfect in integrity of intention. As Miss Edith Lewis, Willa Cather's friend of a lifetime, tells us in a revealing sentence of her book of reminiscences, Willa Cather Living: "The Papal Palace at Avignon . . . stirred her as no building in the world had ever done."

Or we find the pair come out of the glare, resting in grateful shade in the alleys of the papal garden, on its great rock above the rushing river. Another rock, far across the world at Ácoma—in her New Mexican story

—may over the years even stem from this place. The idea of cultivation achieved upon barrenness, of art and labor conquering nature, we can see, appealed strongly.

These hours were retained for life. The oleanders, the almond and lemon trees, the cypress, ilex, and mulberry, every growing thing will leave its mark. And beyond them, like a glittering upper world, tower the cool slopes of the Alps, lovely in color, remote, an ultimate benison. At sunset "they were a pale, pinkish purple, as though all the lilac blossoms that had ever been since the world began had been heaped up there against the hot blue sky." In all these travel articles there is no more impassioned description. Willa Cather is moved by this country! Can it be perhaps because unexpectedly it gave back to her all the simple large values of the West, of her girlhood on the land, yet here sanctioned, translated into history, set nobly and with art against a splendid past, whether of Italy or of France?

The last seven years of Willa Cather's life were passed either in poor health or in bouts with such exhaustion as to make continued work impossible. Yet during all this time, we know, she cherished the idea of making a "nouvelle" with this setting, seen first during these days, as long as forty-five years before. The very name of Avignon, with these fruits of its Provençal soil by some alchemy transplanted to her mind, was to become for her an unfailing sursum corda, so much did it include of what was rich and generous by her own scale of values.

Once we see how she has simply taken it for her own, it comes clear from the text that follows how agreeable it was for the two companions to ramble about, lingering where they would; walking out upon the ruined and famous old bridge, with its pair of Gothic chapels; or back into the shady gardens again; or once more to a height from which they could watch dusk creep over the fertile land, inhaling the spirit of the place until night overtook them.

"Rest and healing," in such descriptions, come not only to "dusty parched Provence," but also to that part of Willa Cather—still, be it remembered, a struggling and unknown schoolteacher from Pittsburgh—which also craved refreshment, and the boon of this fertilization. No wonder, then, that the region was to draw and retain her, by the power of its own genius; and that the values it symbolized were finally to become those to which she was to give her ultimate and perfect, her most mature loyalty.

Avignon, September 3, 1902

WE began our journey south without much enthusiasm, for Paris is a hard place to leave, even when it
rains incessantly and one coughs continually from the
dampness. We left from the Gare de Lyon at night, ar-
riving at Lyon early in the morning. As we had come
to Lyon second-class, having an entire compartment
to ourselves and sleeping quite as comfortably as in a
Pullman sleeping-car, my friend and I felt it our duty
to be economical and to journey down to Avignon
third-class. It seemed, indeed, that all the world was
going south, for there were eight women and one
wretched infant in our compartment, most of them
women of the people and of the soil. Those women of
the soil are all very well in pictures by Millet or Bas-
tien-Lepage, but they are not the most desirable travelling companions in a little compartment on a burning August day, when the mistral is blowing and white
dust hangs heavy on the olive and fig trees. The baby
had not much more clothing on than an infant Bacchus, and its mother was so tired and hot and discour-
aged with life that she threw the infant upon me and
my dress suitcase and left it to its own devices. Next to

my friend sat a German girl who had been shipped
from some town in Prussia and was booked through to
Tarascon. She spoke no French, and was so warm and
stupid that she had much ado to speak German. She
looked very much like a fat pink pig that has been playing in the mud. She wore a heavy stuff dress, and she
had not bathed for many years—all the smelling salts
we had brought with us could not hide that fact. She
had a sort of leather *porte-monnaie* hung about her
neck by a piece of twine. Promptly at one o'clock she
took from this a fat bologna sausage, a lump of black
bread, and a bit of cheese that may have been fresh
when she left her dear Deutschland a week before.
After she had devoured the last of the cheese our trou-
bles were somewhat easier to bear. After all, no trou-
bles of that sort could be really unbearable, with the
Rhone just outside your car window, the Cévennes on
one side of you and the Alps on the other. It is a river
indeed, the Rhone; none of your clear English streamlets that wind through rose-hedged meadows, but a
great green flood of water, sweeping swiftly and
fiercely along between its banks of red clay. On every
hillside were vineyards, a little red and brown now
from the south wind, and above almost every vineyard
the white ruin of one of the castles of the old lords of

Dauphiny. Below Livron the scenery grows constantly more characteristically southern. The soil of the hills is red, the poplars are taller and more slender than in the north, and about all the level plains are the tall black plumes of the cypress, planted there to shield the wretched little patches of melons and Indian corn from the mistral. Everywhere is the glossy green of the fig and the dusty grey of the olive, everywhere the relentless glare of the fervid sun of the Midi. The farmhouses are all low, rambling structures built of cobblestone, with walls four and five feet thick to keep out the heat. The barns and dwellings are all under one roof, with a big open court between, where the wagons and farm implements are kept. All the gardens are hedged with hollyhocks and sunflowers. The whole atmosphere is pervaded by the odour of drying sunflowers. The villages are white clusters of stucco and cobble-stone houses with red-tiled roofs, with grapevines trained above all the windows. Every street is a fine avenue of sycamores. But no matter how dusty the plains, or how stunted the corn, or how swart the olives, there were always and always the pine trees, the faithful sisters of the Rhone, who have followed her down from her blue birthplace up in the cool Alps, and who never leave her, no matter how dwarfed or dusty they become in their southern grape land, until

she flings her impetuous water into the Mediterranean
at last.

At the end of four hours the guard called Avignon,
the signal for our release from the German girl and
her luncheon, and from the infant Bacchus, who was
cutting his teeth and had by this time nearly eaten the
straps off my suitcase. Oh what a thing is a good hotel
at the end of a weary journey, a journey full of heat
and dust and hungry French fleas and people that are
more distasteful than them all! I feel now that I could
spend the rest of my life at this hostelry and ask for
nothing better. It was only after we were comfortably
installed in a room cheerfully papered in red, with
three big gilt mirrors and a famous old writing-table,
the floor tiled in red stone, that I remembered how af-
fectionately Henry James speaks for this particular hotel in one of his essays. It is primitive enough, too; one
takes a bath in a washbasin and goes to bed by candle-
light; but people know how to live in this country. As
we had carried no bologna with us, we were naturally
interested in the dining-room on the afternoon of our
arrival. It happens to be the chapter-room of an ancient church which stood next the hotel several hundred years ago. It is a large hall, with a Gothic ceiling
of arches that spring from columns on each side the

wall, and very old stained-glass windows that throw pools of colour on the white stone floor. On the wall is a great chromo of Napoleon watching the burning of Moscow. Our companions at dinner were half a dozen bachelor merchants of Avignon, some people from Arles, a German professor studying the antiquities of southern France, and several French officers. The dinner consisted of ten courses, each better than the last, with wines that made us sad because we knew we would never taste their like again. Little white fish, just caught in the Rhone and popped into the pan, calf's head with tomato sauce, lamb chops with a wonderful sauce of spinach, big yellow melons and figs and grapes, cream of carrot soup and patties of rice, broiled larks on toast, and marvellous little cakes made of honey and spice and flour. Yet for all this luxury we pay something less than two dollars a day.

How to write of Avignon itself, the fine old city of the popes, I am sure I do not know. Though tourists frequent it so little that we are the only English-speaking people in the place, its history alone would make it one of the most interesting towns in France. When in 1309, because of political complications, Pope Clement V left Italy, he chose Avignon as his residence seat. Until 1377 the popes reigned here, and Avignon was the centre of the Catholic world. Today the papal arms are as much in evidence here as they were six hundred years ago, and everything centres about and is dominated by the papal palace. At the north end of the town there rises an enormous façade of smooth rock three hundred feet above the Rhone. This sheer precipice, accessible from the river side only by winding stone stairways, is crowned by the great palace of the popes. The palace is a huge, rambling Gothic pile, flanked by six square Italian towers, with a beautiful little cathedral in front. The palace faces toward the town, and behind it, overhanging the Rhone, are the popes' gardens. Those popes were luxurious fellows, one would judge, and certainly they were men of taste. Whether they occasionally grew homesick for Italy is not told us, but they brought Italy with them. It must have been an undertaking of some magnitude to make an Italian garden on the top of a bald rock three hundred feet above the Rhone, but there it lies today, as beautiful as when Clement VI planted and watched over it. Four successive terraces rise one from another, each walled with white marble and connected with the terrace above and below it by winding avenues overhung with feathery fir trees, brown with cones. The garden is really a little terraced forest, cool in the hottest noontime and black with shadows. There are hun-

dreds of oleanders as tall as chestnut trees and now
heavy with pink and scarlet blossoms. There are almond trees and black cypresses and tall hedges of ilex
and mulberry and lemon trees with thick, glossy leaves.
There is a fountain, too, and a lake with white swans
on it. But all this is as nothing when one has reached
the topmost terrace and once looked upon the valley
of the Rhone and what lies beyond it. Surely the holy
fathers knew where to build their fine home. Immediately below one lies the white town, with its narrow
streets and red roofs, and the big, rushing, green river.
Beyond that are interminable plains of figs and olives
and mulberries, of poplars and willow hedgerows, with
here and there a wayside cross and its weather-wracked
Christ. Then, to the south, the Cévennes Mountains,
and to the north and east, Alps and Alps and forever
Alps! The first unfolding of it as one mounts the terrace strikes awe to the most phlegmatic soul. It was
late afternoon when we first saw it, and it seemed as
though, besides Avignon and the Rhone, there was
nothing else in the world but the Alps. The clouds
hung about their flanks, but the bases and the peaks
were clear, and the snow gleamed blindingly in the upper gorges. At that hour they were a pale pinkish-pur-
ple, as though all the lilac blossoms that had ever been
since the world began had been heaped up there

against the hot, blue sky. The smell of them, even, seemed to blow to one across the plain. It must have been a fine place for those Italy-loving popes, here where they could always watch the Alps with one eye, and with the other look down upon the Rhone, the great highway to Italy, where every day barges and galleys went leaping down the current to Naples.

At the foot of the cliff, four great stone arches of the famous old Avignon bridge still reach out into the Rhone. There were twenty arches once, when the bridge reached clear across the river to the tower of Philippe le Bel. It was upon this bridge that the young men and maids of Avignon used to dance the farandole on Sundays and at eventime, as Daudet tells in his fine story "The Pope's Mule." It was built by a fraternity of bridge-making friars, and in the third span of the bridge they made two beautiful little chapels of white stone. The clever and talkative old woman who has the bridge in charge now took us out to these chapels and told us many stories of the good old times when the people of Avignon used to dance on the bridge to the tambourine. In the hard stone of the pier there is a green fig tree growing, with no morsel of earth to nourish it, and it clambers up the chapel wall. The seed which grew it was brought down the Rhone once in flood time, so the old woman said. It had begun to grow there, between the crevices of the stone, when she was a girl; and she had lived to see it bear fruit. Ah, the Rhone was a terrible thing in flood time! It entirely covered the island, and only the tips of the Lombard poplars along the shore stuck out of the brown, roaring flood.

The people of Avignon are awake to the beauties of their town. In the afternoon the papal gardens are full of people, but when the cathedral bell rings half past six they disperse to drink a glass in the shady public square before dinner. The sun drops rapidly this far south, and darkness falls as suddenly as though a curtain were suddenly dropped from somewhere. Even while the last sun rays still rest on the high garden, one can see the darkness creeping swiftly over the plains below. It is as though you were looking down on the farms and vineyards through smoked glass. The Alps become a mere dark, irregular line against the horizon. The ilex and cypress trees of the garden of the popes are thick masses of blackness. The scent of the oleanders grows oppressively heavy. The stars come out fast in the blue sky, and the only sound is from the Rhone, that with all its Alp-born impetus rushes past one in the dark.

This, then, is how the days go by in the fine city of the popes. In the morning there is the soup bowl full of chocolate, the hard rolls and pats of fresh butter wrapped in green fig leaves. When we go into the dining-room to get it, Jules arises and puts on a black coat over his suit of white duck, and serves us with ceremony. Then it is time to walk to some of the old feudal ruins perched about on the hills. Through the heat of the day we read in the ilex arbours of the garden above the river. In the late afternoon we watch the changing glories of the Alps until we go off to dine in our Gothic chapter house, and night comes down with rest and healing over dusty, parched Provence.

[12]

Marseilles and Hyères

From Provence the two friends journey to the Riviera, by way of Marseilles. Memories of that story so magical to youth, The Count of Monte Cristo, and further of a young brother whom it once had also enthralled, come back with a sight of the Château d'If. Even in the columns of a newspaper, Willa Cather is very frank about nostalgia. As life goes on, loyalty to the past is to become an ever more important element in her writing. Indeed, the last short story she ever wrote, "The Best Years," is almost surely in part about this same "certain small brother of mine," to whom she had given her heart's affection.

Journeying eastward along the coast, the olive trees command prolonged interest. They become, as it were, a symbol. For the olive, she tells us, "struggles so hard and patiently against circumstances the most adverse, and yet, like the people who love it, manages always to preserve in its contour, no matter how stony the soil, or how heavy the white dust hangs on its leaves, something of grace and beauty."

This is beautiful writing. In allegory it also may serve toward a definition of all Willa Cather's chief characters. Even the most disparate, hard to group together on any other terms, such as Old Mrs. Harris and A Lost Lady, share this hard struggle against odds. Life is so made, as Willa Cather sees it; and the hardy, twisted olive is as good a symbol as any to represent the price all living things must pay for survival.

These hours are rich. Our next interlude is sheer Mediterranean "theater," quite consciously so, a jolly passage from some comic opera, complete even to an extravagantly costumed male chorus. Near midnight the two young women find themselves in a not too reputable quarter of a small seaport, mingling "in the red lights of the café windows" with cheerful, gesticulating sailors. Such jolly company, as one might expect, Willa Cather found exhilarating, and she leaves the scene, for further night travel, regretfully.

Hyères, from a hotel room at dawn the next morning, seems more conventional. This is the Riviera of

over half a century ago, however; and soon we find the
travelers walking out beyond the town, to "have the
world to ourselves with nothing but the pines and
the sea and a book of Provençal poetry." What pleasure to journey thus simply, in a world so uncluttered!

There is one further forecast of interests, in the constant music that accompanies them on this sunny
coast. This enchants her: "Everyone here sings, and
sings musically and tunefully." Here are the Latin
cousins of her later Spanish Johnny with his guitar;
and, wherever she may find them, they evoke a vision
of rich and sanguine living. Here are men, even the
humblest—a house-painter, or an olive-oil merchant—
who evoke true art, merely in the lilt of a melody.
"Last night," she will tell us, "a beggar sang in the
square one of the most beautiful minor airs I ever
heard."

Hyères, September 6, 1902

IT was not until I saw the little white island of the
Château d'If lying out in the sea before the old harbour at Marseilles that I awakened to the fact that we
were at last in Monte Cristo's country, fairly into the

country of the fabulous, where extravagance ceases to exist because everything is extravagant, and where the wildest dreams come true. The road down from Avignon had not been conducive to castle-building, for the rain fell drearily and persistently, and, though this itself is a sort of fairy tale in Provence, it did not stimulate our imagination. But the clouds had broken by the time we looked out from the old harbour at Marseilles and the sunlight played on the white cliffs of the little island, and the first shock produced by the colour of the Mediterranean, coupled with the name of the Château d'If, were enough to heat the fancies that all day had been as wet as the dripping olive trees. Even had the famous state prison not been there, I think the sailors who ran about the harbour would have recalled to me the story in which Dumas put the Arabian Nights to shame. The Château d'If was the beginning of a marked change in our feelings. In a moment one felt the kindling of something that had burned in one long ago, when one lived and suffered and triumphed with Edmond Dantès. The prison and its island, I found, were quite as important to me, quite as hallowed by tradition, quite as moving to contemplate, as Westminster or Nôtre Dame. Aside from the signal importance this island once had for me, I had to consider its attraction for a certain small brother of mine, and bear all his thrills upon me.

Eastward of Marseilles we passed for a long time through the olive country. The fields were small and stony, terraced along the hillsides, and the earth, which had been freely worked about the trees, was as red as brick dust, exactly as a southern painter made it in his fine Provence landscape in the Luxembourg. The longer one stays in the south, the more suggestive the olive tree becomes. It is such a gracious and humble tree; it struggles so hard and patiently against circumstances the most adverse, and yet, like the people who love it, manages always to preserve in its contour, no matter how stony the soil, or how heavy the white dust hangs on its leaves, something of grace and beauty. We journeyed on so through the olive country until evening, now close to the sea, now whirled back into the valleys behind the hills.

Through the complication of an excursion ticket, we were landed at the dockyards of La Seyne, a little shipping town out on the Mediterranean, late at night, with no train leaving for our destination for three hours. We would have spent the night there, but the only discoverable hotel in the place did not tempt us, tired as we were. We alighted from the station omni-

bus about six feet from the edge of the sea, in the heart
of the sailors' quarters. On one side of the narrow, cobble-paved street was a row of sailors' taverns and cafés.
On the other side the Mediterranean itself. Lights of
every colour shone from the freight vessels in the harbour beside us. On each side of this harbour there were
hills that stood out into the water, and beyond them
the open sea. We stood for some moments in the middle of the street, surrounded by a crowd of voluble
sailors, all chattering gaily in the most perplexing dia-
lect. Edmond Dantès was everywhere, dressed exactly
as we have all seen him on the stage, and as we have all
imagined him in our childhood. Wide trousers of white
duck, a navy-blue woollen jacket, the wide braided col-
lar of his light blue cotton shirt reaching outside of his
jacket and over his broad shoulders. He wore military
moustaches, sometimes earrings, a white cotton tam-
o'-shanter with a red tassel at the top, and a red sash
about his waist. There were scores of him all about us.
It occurred to us that some of our friends at home
would be alarmed if they knew that we were standing
in the middle of the sailors' quarter in a Mediterranean shipping town, quite alone, so late at night. But
we saw about us only the most amiable brown faces,
and when we asked where we could find a hotel, not
one, but a score replied. They spoke faster and faster,

and inserted dozens of perplexing expletives; they lined
up and snatched off their caps and pointed out the direction for us, as the chorus of a light opera point and
look expectantly when the strain that introduces the
tenor sounds in the orchestra. A fine tableau they
made, too, in the red lights from the café windows.
The dining-room of the hotel hung over the sea, and
was full of shippers and sailors, with one merchant
from Paris who was the centre of interest. We were
served a very passable sort of dinner by a lightning-
transformation waiter, who attended to twelve people
and did it well. While the shippers were talking of the
prices of things, and the sailors recounting the adventures of the last voyage, and all were pressing each other's hands and patting each other on the shoulder, the
weather took a turn. Very suddenly a boisterous storm
broke over the sea. Blue lightning and wild gusts of
rain, and metallic thunder that rattled rather than
roared, with a great dashing and splashing of water.
For a moment I was perplexed; I had seen just such a
storm as that before somewhere, but where? Finally it
burst upon me, and I remembered well enough. It was
on the stage of the Funke Theatre, when Mr. James
O'Neill used to be sewn up in a sack and flung by the
supers from the Château d'If into the Mediterranean.
This was exactly such a harmless, spectacular storm; a

stage storm, a mere fit of Mediterranean temper that explodes in a stiletto, and then melts away into smiles and tears. About two hours later we got a train out for Hyères, and I have left many a more attractive place with less regret than this rough little seaport where we were thrown by chance. Next morning we were awakened at five o'clock in our comfortable hotel chamber at Hyères by the fierce glare of a tropical sun, rising over the tops of the date palms.

Hyères is one of the oldest health resorts on the Mediterranean, and in the winter is much frequented by English people. There is even an English bank here, which is open for two hours on two days in the week. So far, however, we have met no one who speaks English except a little black Provençal, who has a large sign, "English Pharmacie; English Spoken," over the door of his shop. We went and addressed him in that tongue, and the little man was covered with confusion. He blushed crimson and hung his head, and muttered guiltily, *"Un peu anglaise je parle,* Miss." Hyères itself is a red-roofed town that hangs on the side of a steep pine-clad hill above the sea. All the streets are shaded by date palms and giant eucalyptus trees, and the powdery mimosa trees of Algiers and the desert. The fields in the valley below grow all the roses and violets that

Paris wears in the wintertime. Not a night at the opera that the violets of Hyères, grown here in this limpid air and warm sea wind, are not worn by the beautiful women of the capital. Then there are olive orchards, and about them all the blossoming hedges of oleander. Below Hyères the scented pine hills slope down to the sea, very high hills, covered with scrub pine and fir trees that grow with straight stems, and no branches at all until they suddenly flare out wide at the top, like big green umbrellas. There is no beach at all: six feet from the pine trees is the sea, as still and motionless as a plaque of blue porcelain, with a sky of enamel above it. In the distance the hills are a pale violet. The still water is cut here and there by sailboats, sweeping along in their blue furrows with the swiftness of boats in a fairy tale. Some of them have white sails, others salmon pink, such as the boats of Venice that Zeim so often paints. All the sailors wear white caps and red sashes, and they all sing. Everyone here sings, and sings musically and tunefully. The young house-painter at work on our hotel sings airs from *Rigoletto* all day as he works, the olive-oil buyer across the way rumbles the choruses from *Trovatore* in a sonorous bass, like a big bumblebee, as he goes to the post office. Last night a beggar sang in the square one of the most beautiful minor airs I ever heard, and always and everywhere one

hears the *L'Arlésienne* of Bizet. Bizet lives still in Provence, though they know his *L'Arlésienne* better even
than *Carmen*.

The beach is almost deserted at this season of the
year. We walk about four miles from town and have
the world to ourselves, with nothing but the pines
and the sea and a book of Provençal poetry. Far away,
on the hilltops, is the white ruin of a castle that the
Saracens held in the tenth and eleventh centuries, and
which was later the stronghold of a band of pirates
who ravaged the coast and terrorized the sea. But my
purpose is not to tell here of the beauties of Hyères,
only to suggest the lightning transformations and
magical changes that may occur in a land that is a sort
of Christmas pantomime for scenery. What more of
life could one wring out of twenty-four hours, if you
please? At noon the wet olives of Arles; at nightfall a
chorus of gay sailors, made up to the life, and the rattle
of stage thunder, much blue lightning, and a great toss-
ing of blue water; at dawn a sunrise over feathery date
palms, with the sea at one's feet and a porcelain sky
above. What more could one ask for, even in the country of Monte Cristo?

[13]

Le Lavandou

At the beginning of this second article on her Mediterranean days, Willa Cather tells us that she has chosen to visit an unknown and quiet little fishing village on purpose. She had sought it out; this is typical of her way of travel. Here, amid a mere score of the humblest houses, set on barren land beside a "smiling, niggardly sea," is the simple accommodation that was all she wanted. Emptiness was her present need.

She was of course fortunate in finding such an open, unspoiled region. In 1902 she can still tell us how "the coast for a hundred miles on either side of us is quite as wild as it was when the Saracens held it." There is only one small train a day, on narrow-gauge tracks; no airplanes yet existed, to drone overhead in the limpid "sky of porcelain."

She needed rest, of course, perhaps even more than she herself knew. In Pittsburgh, to all the fatigues of the busy school year she had been adding serious efforts to write, to compose, in free time. And now upon these she had piled exciting and strenuous travel. Here, then, was a chance for utter cessation of effort. Here life made, for once, no demands; and also for the moment she need not make any of herself. Here was that rarity in her own life: surcease.

"One cannot divine nor forecast the conditions that will make happiness," she tells us; "one only stumbles upon them by chance, in a lucky hour, at the world's end somewhere, and holds fast to the days, as to fortune or fame." So we find her deeply grateful: "Nothing else in England or France has given anything like this sense of immeasurable content." With insight she sees how this quiet, this rustic charm, have ministered even to heart's ease.

For their sunlit hours of repose, the two young women take possession of the grounds of a small, empty, near-by villa. Here, beside the glassy sea, they can sit the long day through; in perfect repose at last, lost in space, in the simple elements of earth and sky, the soughing of the pines, and blue water. Here the cisterns of the spirit can slowly fill once more.

Willa Cather's sense of her riches is great. There is

even unconscious pathos in her unexpected vocabulary to describe the idle hours. Struggle is, for the moment, over; she can taste the rare luxury of possession by right rather than by effort. So she refers handsomely to her "fair demesne of lavender tufts"; to her "regal idleness"; or her "royal progress" from her "principality of pines"—to a near-by village. We even find "neighbouring princesses," two diminutive girls, seriously pasturing their family goat, cajoling it, talking to it. The little scene has great charm. It also shows a side of her nature she will not often turn to us. Here, wonderfully, living involves no strife; this is a fairy tale!

Yet the treasure will not last. She knows that, after only a little, burdens—even if those of new assimilation —will have to be resumed. She is obligated to press on again, to Nice and Monte Carlo; "proof enough," she concludes, "that one cannot become really acclimated to happiness."

Le Lavandou, September 10, 1902

WE came to Lavandou chiefly because we could not find anyone who had ever been here, and because in Paris people seemed never to have heard of the place.

It does not exist on the ordinary map of France, and Baedeker, in his *Southern France,* merely mentions it. Lavandou is a fishing village of less than a hundred souls, that lies in a beautiful little bay of the Mediterranean. Its score or so of houses are built on the narrow strip of beach between the steep hillside and the sea. They are scarcely more than huts, built of mud and stone on either side of one narrow street. There is one café, and before it is a little square of sycamore trees, where the sailors, always barefoot, with their corduroy trousers and tam-o'-shanter caps, play some primitive game of ball in the afternoon. There is one very fairly good hotel, built on the sea, and from the windows of our rooms we have the whole sweep of ocean before us. There is a long veranda running the full length of the house on the side facing the sea, straw-thatched and overgrown by gourd vines, where all our meals are served to us. The fare is very good for a semi-desert country, though the wine here is thin and sour and brackish, as though the sea-wash had got into the soil that grew it. The wine of the country just here is all red, for the white grapes which flourish about Avignon grow poorly here. We have good fish, however, excellent sauces, plenty of fresh figs and peaches, and the fine little French lobster called *langouste.* Every morning the one little train that rattles in over the narrow-gauge tracks from Hyères brings us our piece of ice, done up in a bit of sailcloth, and we watch for it eagerly enough. This little train constitutes our railroad service, and it comprises a toy engine, a coal car, a mail and baggage car, and two coaches, one for first and one for second class.

The coast for a hundred miles on either side of us is quite as wild as it was when the Saracens held it. It is one endless succession of pine hills that terminate in cliffs jutting over the sea. There are no cattle or pigs raised here, and the people drink only goat's milk besides their own wines. The gardens are for the most part pitiful little hillside patches of failure. Potatoes, figs, olives, and grapes are almost the only things that will grow at all in this dry, sandy soil. The sea is an even more uncertain harvest, as, with the exception of the lobsters, the fish of the Mediterranean are not particularly good, and bring a low price in the market. The water, indeed, is not cold enough to produce good fish. How the people live at all I am not able to discover. They burn pine knots and cones for fuel—the thermometer never goes down to freezing-point—and they are able to make a savoury dish of almost anything that grows. They are very fond of a salad they make of little sea-grass, dressed with the oil they get from their olives. But never imagine they are not happy, these poor fishermen of this smiling, niggardly sea. Every day we see them along the road as we walk back to the village; before every cottage the table set under an arbour or under an olive tree, with the family seated about, eating their figs and sea-grass salad, and drinking their sour wine, and singing—always singing.

Out of every wandering in which people and places come and go in long successions, there is always one place remembered above the rest because the external or internal conditions were such that they most nearly produced happiness. I am sure that for me that one place will always be Lavandou. Nothing else in England or France has given anything like this sense of immeasurable possession and immeasurable content. I am sure I do not know why a wretched little fishing village, with nothing but green pines and blue sea and a sky of porcelain, should mean more than a dozen places that I have wanted to see all my life. No books have ever been written about Lavandou, no music or pictures ever came from here, but I know well enough that I shall yearn for it long after I have forgotten London and Paris. One cannot divine nor forecast the conditions that will make happiness; one only stumbles upon them by chance, in a lucky hour, at the world's end somewhere, and holds fast to the days, as to fortune or fame.

About a mile down the shore from the village there is a little villa of white stucco, with a red-tiled roof and a little stone porch, built in the pines. It is the winter studio of a painter who is in Paris now. He has managed to keep away from it all the disfiguring and wearisome accompaniments of houses made with hands. There is no well, no stable, no yard, no driveway. It is a mere lodge, set on a little table of land between two cliffs that run out into the sea. All about it are the pines, and the little porch and plateau are covered with pine needles. You approach it by a winding path that runs down through the underbrush from the high-road. There, for the last week, we have taken up our abode. Nominally we stopped at the Hôtel de la Méditerrané, but we only slept and ate there. For twelve hours out of the twenty-four we were the possessors of a villa on the Mediterranean, and the potentates of a principality of pines. There is before the villa a little plateau on the flat top of a cliff extending out into the sea, brown with pine needles, and shaded by one tall, straight pine tree that grows on the very tip of the little promontory. It is good for one's soul to sit there all the day through, wrapped in a steamer rug if the sea breeze blows strong, and to do nothing for hours together but stare at this great water that seems to trail its delft-blue mantle across the world. Then, as Daudet said, one becomes a part of the foam that drifts, of the wind that blows, and of the pines that answer.

Besides having a manor, we have a demesne as well, a fair demesne of lavender tufts that grow thick over the hills; and their odourous blossoms, drying in the sun, mingle their fresh, salt perfume with the heavier odour of the pines. Our only labour is to gather these blossoms; but so regal is our idleness that we have much ado to accomplish it.

Going to and fro, we have made the acquaintance of certain neighbouring princes and princesses whose kingdoms lie round about. There are, in the first place, two little girls, whom we meet every day seeking pasture for their goat. As the goat supplies the milk and butter for the family, it is most necessary that she should have good grass; and that, on this arid coast, is not easy to find in September. When they have found a green spot, they carefully tether her, and with many parting injunctions to her not to run away, and to eat all she can, and be a good little goat, they leave her. Then there is the old man who lives in a thatch on the hillside, from whom we buy figs; and the woman who goes about with scales and basket, selling lobsters. At the hotel there is an old Parisian who has exiled himself from the gaieties of the capital, and is living out the remainder of a misspent life in the solitudes of his native south. His eyes fairly devour anyone who comes from Paris, and he beams when a bicyclist or two pump into Lavandou to solace his loneliness. For several days he has been the only guest at the hotel besides ourselves, and he eats his lobster and sips his benedictine in sadness.

The other day we left our manor long enough to make a royal progress to Cavalaire, a village six miles down the coast. The road is a wild one: on one side the steep hillside, on the other the sea. If we had not tested the kindliness of these southerners before, we might have been rather intimidated by the loneliness of the road. We met nothing more terrible than a sailor boy sitting on the stone coping of a bridge, trying to tie up a badly bruised foot in a piece of cloth torn from the sash about his waist. He had been put ashore that morning off a freight boat because his foot disabled him, and was limping along to St. Praid, twenty-five miles down the coast, where his people lived. He did not ask for charity, nor vouchsafe his story until he was questioned. We gave him some money, and a pin to keep the cloth on his foot, and as we were returning late in the afternoon, we met him limping on his way. We met also a few fishermen, and several women walking beside little carts drawn by a donkey no bigger than a sheep, and every woman was knitting busily as she walked, stopping only long enough to greet us. The village of Cavalaire consists of a station house and a little tavern by the roadside. The station agent lay asleep on a bench beside his door, and his old mother and wife were knitting beside him. The place is not a little like certain lonely way stations in Wyoming and Colorado. Before we reached our own village that night the moon was already throwing her tracks of troubled light across the sea.

But always we come back to the principality of pines and decide there is nothing else quite so good. As I said before, there is nothing but a little cardboard house of stucco, and a plateau of brown pine needles, and green fir trees, the scent of dried lavender always in the air, and the sea reaching like a wide blue road into the sky. But what a thing it is to lie there all day in the fine breeze, with the pine needles dropping on one, only to return to the hotel at night so hungry that the dinner, however homely, is a fête, and the menu finer reading than the best poetry in the world! Yet we are to leave all this for the glare and blaze of Nice and Monte Carlo; which is proof enough that one cannot become really acclimated to happiness.

[14]

Arles and Provence Again

To anyone familiar with the work of Willa Cather, it is interesting to observe how through a whole lifetime she is never attracted by conventional splendor. The greatest monuments, the historic palaces of the past— with the single and notable exception of the great building in Avignon—draw her far less than humble dwellings. Toil, not ease, was the natural element in which she moved; sooner or later all the rest seems merely to bore her.

Monte Carlo serves as a good example; and here she analyzes her own feelings revealingly. All is simply too luxurious, too complete. Here, as she puts it, she finds "no life at all that takes hold upon the soil or grapples with the old conditions set for a people." The setting is factitious. So she is far from reluctant to depart, to return to her real world, back to Provence and Daudet's country again. For life on the Riviera, thus artificially embellished, there is cool dismissal.

In Arles, bright but suddenly autumnal, she is immediately active once more, seeming to know as by instinct how such a region lives, whence flow the sources of its daily life. Rapidly she achieves a vivid reconstruction of the local pattern, animating the rustic setting with her usual gift, sketching out for us a whole cycle of rich Provençal living. Those who have read Death Comes for the Archbishop and Shadows on the Rock can here trace rudiments of a technique that she will bring to perfection only after many years.

In Arles, however, September has now arrived; and with it even a pang of homesickness. Changes of color that come with the autumn, a chill once more in the evening air—these remind her of other days, at home. Again we find her turning with nostalgia toward old times, toward the old ways in both lands. Modern materialism with all its "goblin" activities, no matter where she encounters them, are her natural enemies; this is a conviction that will only deepen with living. Part of her definite philosophy we thus find here in embryo.

It is easy to see why an earthbound pastoral people,

with deep-rooted local pride, and also with a natural gift for verse, for song, would strongly attract her. The patriarchal vintners, in their solid houses among the vines; the troubadours, old or young; the splendid ample women bearing proudly their great classical heritage, even in the channels of the blood—all make daily living in Provence rich in the only way that Willa Cather ever really cared to enrich it.

Conscientiously, at this point she throws into her article a few guidebook facts; although soon she begins further speculation, on life in this region under the Romans; and this too—almost in spite of herself—she must attempt to reconstruct, once more using her materials plastically.

By this time, though, we are also able to appraise her own development over the course of the summer, as she easily handles the rich time-scales of Old World life, contrasting one country with another, divining Rome behind the Middle Ages. How much she has matured since the first days of her arrival in "quaint" Chester, merely a matter of weeks before!

Such rapid growth can become painful; and there is an almost disquieting quality to the theorizing into which she now suddenly falls. Where and how, we wonder, did she acquire the sweeping conclusions about Latin decline and Northern ascendancy to which she suddenly submits us, and which we can see have gripped her tenaciously? A prey to them for the moment, however—although their hold does not seem to have become permanent—with her customary vigor she dismisses Latin culture as beautiful but doomed, and then somewhat unexpectedly reverts to England to close her series.

So we are transferred to London, to Hyde Park on a day of splendid military pageantry. On the greensward is the armed might of Britain; and also a crowd of fascinated young children, who in their turn will become her warriors. As these last are irresistibly drawn to the splendid horses of the cavalry, symbolic of what life will hold for them, she first quotes Kipling and then even waves a Union Jack at us, to close. Never say that here we have not an independent spirit!

This may be a prefiguration, a premonition; one, moreover, on a very large scale. For in her own life Willa Cather was first fascinated, even in Nebraska, by all her neighbors who were not Anglo-Saxons, by every foreign element she could find. In the beginning, all of these other cultures seemed to her to possess more beauty and color, to provide more enrichment for daily living, than the one to which she by birth belonged.

Then, as life went on, she apparently was slowly drawn better to appreciate the virtues of her own race.

At the end, even—having moved, for her setting, first to the Spanish Southwest and then to the French Northeast of her own continent—for her last novel she returned to her native Virginia, of a time not long preceding her own birth. In Sapphira and the Slave Girl the chief characters, besides the slaves, will be her own people.

One must not press the conclusion to extremes. Willa Cather never lost her love for what was fine in the immigrants. Certainly, also, she was working further on a story about people in just this part of France, even up to the time of her death. Perhaps, then, life effected a broadening rather than a diminution of her sympathies; and she probably never tried to define these by permanent exclusion.

Yet here, on this first journey, she apparently felt compelled to deliver herself of some recapitulation at its close, to spread broad on the page something of what she felt after these so full, so developing and disturbing weeks of heady travel. And it may have taken more strength than even she, at this time, possessed, to take a balanced view, altogether to avoid invidious comparison.

It is typical of her, though, not to sidestep the problem. Even in these fugitive columns of hasty travel notes she seems to have felt deeply that she must in

some way come to grips with it. Her present theories
may be impermanent, but her old, high values are not.
There must be no compromise with fundamentals; and
one must have abiding standards. Also, one must state
conclusions even as one finds them.

Arles, September 16, 1902

IT is with something like a sigh of relief that one
quits the oppressive splendour of Monte Carlo to re-
trace one's steps back into Daudet's country. I am sure
I do not know why the beauty of Monte Carlo should
not satisfy more than it does. The bluest of all seas is
nowhere bluer than when you see it between the marble balustrades of the long white terrace before the casino, palms are nowhere greener than in that high garden which the mountains screen from every unkind
breath, no colours could be more rich and various than
those of the red and purple Alps that tower up behind
the town, on whose summits such violent thunder-
storms gather and break. But for me, at least, there was
not at all the pleasure I had anticipated in this dazzling
white and blue, these feathery palms and ragged Alps.
It is a common experience that, in pleasant dreams,

when conditions are approaching to perfection, when the work long undone is done, or the friend who has so long been bitter grows kind, with this flood of exultation there comes the conviction, "This is a dream." I had a continual restless feeling that there was nothing at all real about Monte Carlo; that the sea was too blue to be wet, the casino too white to be anything but pasteboard, and that from their very greenness the palms must be cotton. It may be that other things, as well as the superb stage settings of the place, go to produce this effect. Though all Europe goes to spend its money in this little kingdom not three miles long, there is nothing at all produced or manufactured there, and no life at all that takes hold upon the soil or grapples with the old conditions set for a people. In atmosphere and spirit the entire kingdom of Monaco is an extension of the casino.

A day's riding through red earth and olives and miles of vineyard lands where the grape-pickers are busy brought us back to middle Provence, the heart of Daudet's country. The country of tambourines and Muscat wine, he calls it, and the phrase is more presentive than a volume of close description. It is a high, windy, dusty country, just anchored on the banks of the turbulent Rhone, where the mistral continually threatens to dislodge it and blow it away. The mistral is a fierce reality now, it buffets us like a gale at sea, more terrible than any wind that ever came up from Kansas. The fig trees are powdered with white dust until they are all but as grey as the olives, the vineyards are red as October oak leaves, the smell of drying fruit, of ripe things, and of making wine is everywhere. Even in Arles the sycamore leaves are beginning to turn a little, and over her narrow streets in the evening there falls the chill of autumn, the strange, homesick chill that always makes one want to be home, where there are geraniums to be potted for winter and little children to be got ready for school. But in the daytime one forgets these things in the excitement of continual novelty, and who could be gloomy on a September morning at Arles? The town could never have retained its colour and quaintness had it been in any touch with modern commerce, but Arles is the centre of a large pastoral district, a great country of shepherd kings and farmer barons, of fat priests, of old customs and simple living. Every one of these stone farmhouses, stable and dwelling together, with the farmyard court between, is a sort of feudal manor. Usually three generations and many servants live there: the grandparents, the married son who has inherited the farm, his children, and the wagoners and shepherds. No farmer has a desire to be anything else, or to live in any better house than the one his father lived in, or to see a larger city than Arles. They keep carefully all their ancient festivals, the Noël and the feasts of their patron saints and name saints. They desire to live honourably and long, to marry their daughters well, and to have strong sons to succeed them, to avoid innovation and change, to drink their Muscat wine and eat their boiled snails and tomatoes fried in oil to the end. The word of the master is the only law needed; the women sit down to meat only after the men are served. When a child is born, his godmother stands at the four corners of his bed holding salt, bread, eggs, and wine. If he have always enough of those, that is quite enough to wish for him. Simple ambitions these seem for this century, but they express nearly the whole will and need of the people of Provence, who are a truly pastoral people still. Besides being shepherds and farmers, almost every Provençal is a poet. The gallery of the portraits of native poets at Arles represents several hundred poets, and the unpublished rhymesters are of course even more numerous. They make songs as they make wine down in this country; it grows up from this old red soil that bred the first troubadours ages since, it distills from the pines, it breaks from the red grapes. Boys come into some knack of song-making as they come into long trousers, as they come into the age when they go a-courting. It is natural, and makes no great stir unless it develops to a higher degree of perfection, as it did in Daudet. The shepherds make songs in the mountains as they watch their flocks at night, the grandfather sings by the fire on winter nights the songs he made in his youth, and the grandson sings to some Arlésienne the song he made yesterday.

The women of Arles alone might well account for the songful bent of their country. They are noted all over France for their beauty, which is of a rather Moorish type, and now and then strangely Roman. Their clear-cut features, olive skin, oval faces, and fine, full eyes are well set off by their costume of velvet and lace, their fine fichus brought low about their bare brown throats, and their lace and ribbon caps on their blue-black hair. Their splendid, generous figures are an especial point of pride with them. Surely if poor Mrs. Fiske had ever been to Arles and come and gone among these splendid brown creatures for a time, she would never have found the courage to produce Daudet's *L'Arlésienne*.

We are not fortunate enough to see a bullfight at Arles, as they occur only on Sunday and we cannot

stay over. The bulls for the ring are reared in a deso-
late, fever-stricken, marshy land called the Camargue.
The only intruders on this reedy wilderness are the
herdsmen, the duck-hunters, and the mistral. The
herdsmen live there from year's end to year's end, "and
their existence is so solitary," Daudet remarks, "that
when they come to town once or twice a year, the little
cafés of Arles seem to them more magnificent than the
palaces of the Ptolemies." The bullfights still take
place in the old Roman amphitheatre, built in this rich
colonial town in the first Christian century. This amphitheatre is one of the most extensive Roman ruins in
France, and is in a much better state of preservation
than the Colosseum at Rome. It is five hundred yards
in circumference, and contains forty-three tiers of
seats. It originally held twenty-six thousand people, but
so numerous are the exits that the house could be
emptied of this crowd in four minutes. The edifice at
present looks as though it might last until the end of
time, as long as the Latin tongue is echoed anywhere.
The ravages of the years are but little apparent; it is
still as huge and white under its blue porcelain sky as
it was in the days of Constantine, and even the loftiest
Gothic seems small beside its stubborn, arrogant, de-
fiant hugeness.

.   .   .

The tragic theatre, though ill-preserved, is quite as impressive. The white ledge on which the auditors sat remains, though stained and broken. The stone box about the pit from which the curtain rose is intact, but only two remain of the twenty splendid marble columns which stood so slenderly against the sky and formed a noble background for the toga-clad players. Why is it that neither Daudet nor Flaubert nor Gautier ever attempted to give us a study of the civilization of those proud old Roman colonies? In the south it seems quite as though the living tie between France and her mother country had never been cut. This ruined theatre, its marble sunk in turf and overgrown with mild mustard and candytuft, seems a legitimate part of Provence, a growth of its own soil. What an active and vigorous life the colonists must have lived here in their Arelate, as they called it, in the days when Constantine built his palace by the Rhone. The wreck of that palace is still here, wind-wracked and flood-wracked but unmistakable. A wonderful liking the Romans had for the Gothic soil they had subdued; they liked the climate, the wines, the remoteness from the turbulent political strife of Italy. They made a continual effort to recall Italy in the architecture, dress, and social life of their colony. They called Arelate the "Gallic Rome," and adorned her with theatres and baths and a forum, just as the cities of the French provinces today copy Paris. These colonists had a sort of Chicago-like vehemence in adorning their city and making it ostentatiously rich. They sent their artists to Rome to be trained, and gave them enough to do on their return. Every galley that came up the Rhone from Naples brought masterpieces of weaving, sculpture, painting, or pottery, and musicians and actors who came to the colonies to play in the summer season, when the heat of southern Italy drove playgoers to the Apennines. The famous Venus of Arles in the Louvre at Paris was originally brought from Rome to grace the foyer of the theatre, and was found there in 1651. Before the theatre was a fountain, Silenus reclining on a fat wine-skin, from the open mouth of which the jet of water played. This fountain is now preserved in the museum at Arles. The theatre was begun in the reign of Augustus, and the head of the Emperor which stood in the foyer is certainly the finest portrait I have ever seen of him, though they are in every museum in Europe. There is an equally fine head of Livia, which stood by that of her husband, and one of the little Marcellus, erected before his death, when he was still the hope and pride of the empire. There is an interesting head, too, of the infant Constantine, grave and devout as a little St. John. But of all the sculptures which have been found in this old town that the Latins made so fair, the most beautiful is a triplex bas-relief that was placed in the wall of their theatre. The middle section represents the triumph of the poet: laurel-crowned, the Muses behind him, calmness and dignity upon his brow, striking his lyre with all the confidence of mastery. At the left is a smaller scene, a single figure, Apollo, sharpening his knife on a stone. At the right is another picture with but one figure, Marsyas, the poet of the middle panel, hanging from an oak tree by his thonged hands, his skin hanging limp and wet about his flayed limbs, his broken lyre at his feet. Surely it was a frank fashion these Romans had of encouraging their tragic poets!

After one spends a day or two among the Roman remains in the museums here, the portrait busts and mosaics and beautifully sculptured tombs, it seems almost as if there may be some truth in the old story that the women of Arles owe their beauty to the vows they used to make to their pagan Venus in secret, and that their children come into the world with the fine, clear profiles that are cut on the old Roman tombs. In Italy itself one could scarcely feel more the presence of Rome, of the empire and all it meant, of its self-devouring and suicidal vastness, than here in the land where the richest and proudest of its colonies flourished. One sunny afternoon we were examining some broken columns and fragments of capitals tumbled beside a wall of turf and overgrown with white candytuft, which makes the air sweet and keeps the bees coming and going. The finest thing we found was a section of a cornice, perhaps six feet long, with a great eagle upon it, a garland in his beak. The eagle, the one and only eagle, here in the far corner of the earth where the shadow of his great wings falls, the one bird more terrible in history than all the rest of brute creatures put together. Above him was the inscription "Rome Eternal." Yet they say that even the most remote of his descendants are doomed, that all who echo his tongue and bear his blood must perish, and that these fine, subtle, sensitive, beauty-making Latin races are rotten at heart and must wither before the cold wind from the north, as their mothers did long ago. Whoever is a reasonable being must believe it, and whoever believes it must regret it. A life so picturesque, an art so rich and so divine, an intelligence so keen and flexible—and yet one knows that this people face toward the setting, not the rising, sun.

I was in London several months ago when Lord Kitchener and his troops returned from Africa. On the day of the commander's arrival, after the procession from Paddington, and while the reception at St. James's was in progress, there were several thousand cavalry horses picketed in Hyde Park. There was a tramping of red coats everywhere, and the trains of rajahs from the east were moving this way and that, glittering in gold and crimson, the nobles of a conquered race. But the spirit of that day lay not in these things. Before those thousands of horses there were rows and rows of children, children who had clambered out of carriages, children who had clambered out of gutters, children who seemed to have sprung from a sowing of the dragon's teeth; and they were all petting and stroking the animals with a pride, an earnestness, a wistfulness touching to see. There they were: "Duke's son, cook's son, son of a hundred kings," each whispering a vow to the horses of the cavalry. One felt in a flash of conviction from what blood the world's masters were to come. The poet of the line said that "On the bones of the English the English Flag is stayed." From the time the Englishman's bones harden into bones at all, he makes his skeleton a flagstaff, and he early plants his feet like one who is to walk the world and the decks of all the seas.